IGNITING THE FLAME OF OUR DIVINE HUMANITY

SACRED BODY
WISDOM

with featured authors

RIMA BONARIO ⚲ ZAHAVA GRISS ⚲ ROCHELLE SCHIECK ⚲ LETTIE SULLIVAN

WITH ESSAYS FROM 16 NEW PARADIGM LEADERS | COMPILED BY JANE ASHLEY

FLOWER *of* LIFE PRESS.

W9-CMN-151

PRAISE

"*Lainie Love Dalby, it has been powerful to read your essay in* Sacred Body Wisdom, *with your story, passion and purpose. I have not read such honest, living, generative material in a long time. It definitely brought me deep into my own journey and history. I connect with your story from my own experience of separation and disconnection within my body and it is so real and painful, I am just relieved you are speaking your truth about it. I so respect and appreciate your stand for truth and authenticity. Your words and expression are powerful medicine for the world.*"

—R.M.

"*As a man reading Eden's journey I was in for a ride I didn't expect. A master story teller, Eden courageously invites you into an intimate reflection of the reclamation of her sacred body wisdom. You will not only become fully engaged in her compelling heroines journey but also be immersed in a powerful shamanic journey in the process. With the precision of a diamond cutter, Eden empowers us to sculpt through the illusion of comparative thinking and limiting beliefs to walk in honor and celebration of our innate beauty. Eden's awareness supersedes gender identification and serves as a powerful tool for personal transformation.*"

—John Burgos, International Speaker, author and Host of Beyond The Ordinary Show

"*In* Sacred Body Wisdom, *Lynette Cannon takes us on a hypnotic journey of internal separation and re-integration. She eloquently explores the sometimes painful process of facing our deepest wounds and the stories surrounding them. Through the description of personal process, acknowledging our inner-child separation, and drawing on the power of Divine Feminine Wisdom, Lynette nudges us to seek, question, respond, and take responsibility for the stories surrounding our wounds. Leading us to acknowledge the ultimate love and power that we have inside of us to heal ourselves...if we listen, respond, and remember.*"

—Michelle Miller, Healing with Spirit

"*In* Sacred Body Wisdom, *Nadia Munla recounts her heartbreaking and triumphant story with raw and utterly compelling candor. Her staggering resilience, fortitude, and transformation is nothing short of inspirational. She is an absolute marvel of a spirit and shaman with a gift of inner alchemy.*"

—Julian DeVoe, author of *Robust Vitality* and *Insights Out*

"*In* Sacred Body Wisdom, *Zahava Griss offers a powerful point of entry into what it means to honor, appreciate and build sacred, loving, and inclusive community. It is kindling for the willing—may it spark dialogue everywhere.*"

—Rha Goddess, Entrepreneurial Soul Coach, CEO of Move The Crowd

"*In* Sacred Body Wisdom, *Dr. Mara Sussman beautifully shares an experience of healing the soul by looking deeper. This is the way of the Shaman, to look deeper, past the illusion for answers, healing, and purpose. As we learn to do this individually, so it will be collectively. Our challenges are gifts and our healing process with them is Sacred. Kudos to Mara for breaking beyond fear and doubt, for delving deeper and reclaiming her power!*"

—Dr. Kara Hanks, NHD, RN, HHP, Shaman, Spiritual Healer, Leader, and Educator

"*In* Sacred Body Wisdom, *Bernadette Pleasant's chapter 'Hips Don't Lie' is highly engaging—like a picture that she paints with her feelings. I went on the journey with her. It was actually hard to sit still as she described how she was physically and emotionally moved by the power of movement. I was inspired by how she not only found a way to liberate herself, but used that experience to help other people do the same. Her story left me wanting more. It made me curious and made me want to experience what she described—in my own body!*"

—Karen A. Chambers, Executive VP, IMAN Cosmetics

"*Aurora Farber's essay about the Magic of the Moon has helped my own feminine abundance journey immensely! I am so grateful and glad for all of her incredible goddess aura and medicine...reading her story gives me an inspiring framework and understanding for the ancient wisdom that is embedded in all of our DNA. At The Gut Institute, I work with men and women to reduce fatigue, fat, and brain fog in six months or less and one of the primary tenets for the women is achieving our 29-day lunar cycle. Most women tell me they never thought this was possible. When they do, they are totally shocked to know that all of their life-long PMS, clotty menstrual cycles, tender breasts, migraines, fatigue, fibroids, and aches all go away as well! Thank you for all that you do Aurora and for shedding moonlight on four different aspects of being feminine, nurturing, and happy!*"

—Dr. Grace Liu, PharmD AFMCP, Functional Medicine
Practitioner & Gut Health Educator, www.TheGutInstitute.com

"*In* Sacred Body Wisdom, *Shannon Lee's story may sound familiar to many of us. It certainly rang loud and clear with me since I have experienced many of the same feelings throughout my life. Besides being professionally qualified to help empower others, Shannon Lee's life experiences are what make her an outstanding health coach. Give yourself an incredible gift and spend some time with Shannon Lee and allow her to help you love yourself.*"

—Tracy P Marti

"In Sacred Body Wisdom, *Jeanne Adwani illustrates what happens when the fearless are confronted with aging and ageism. She reclaims her sexuality out loud, challenging society to see age for what it is: the beauty that can only come from wisdom and confidence."*

—Penni Jones, author of *On the Bricks* and *Kricket*

"Woman, your story in Sacred Body Wisdom: Igniting the Flame of Our Divine Humanity *is potent, vulnerable ALIVENESS. I felt myself nodding, laughing, and heart-twisting my way through every word. Nadia, thank you for baring your soul journey. I feel more connected to my own, more trusting in the messy magic of becoming."*

—Rachael Maddox, author of *Secret Bad Girl*

"Rima's is a deeply moving, inspiring story of transformation and awakening. Through the power of Shakti she fell in love with her body. She discovered pleasure and a home in the body she had spent a lifetime loathing and feeling betrayed by. She shares practical wisdom and solutions for many of our most challenging issues as women. And she spoke to so many human challenges we face as women in our relationship with our bodies, whether it's familial or religious messages, childhood trauma or the trials of puberty. I highly recommend this powerful story."

—Joni Advent Maher, Creator of Revolutionary Heart

"Bernadette Pleasant always knows how to speak to the depths of my soul. Her shared wisdom evokes a knowingness within that wakes me up and puts me at ease at the same time. She is a magician that way. Reading her words I feel like, 'Oh yeah, she's been there, she knows the way, and oh, maybe I do, too! There's hope!' The way she shows up in the world is raw, uncompromising, and altogether brimming with selfless compassion. Take note: Her words are powerful. There are no good, bad, light, or dark emotions. Only emotions that need to be fully expressed."

—Laura V.

"Aurora Farber's chapter, "Voices in the Moonlight" is a hauntingly beautiful and powerful read, evoking many memories and feelings I've experienced in my own life. Although I have not thought about the moon in a long time, I am inspired by the poetic verses Aurora offers for each moon phase. These feminine "voices" are so rich and powerful...I am going to refer to these when I do my daily morning journal writing. Thank you, Aurora, for your open, raw, courageous, and beautiful sharing. You have deeply touched me!"

—Debbie DiPietro, author of *Short Morning Prayers*,
Podcast Host of Courageously Go!, CourageouslyGo.com

FLOWER OF LIFE PRESS.
Voices of Transformation

I finally realized that being grateful to my body
was key to giving more love to myself.

—Oprah Winfrey

SIPPING ON STARDUST

Artist: Lainie Love Dalby
Medium: Mixed media shamanic healing collage, 2018

I believe in the power of art making itself as a form of prayer, deep healing, and communion with the divine. It is a vehicle for the secret language of the soul that helps lure us back to wholeness. That's why I refer to my shamanic healing pieces as he(art)works. The expressive arts help us to access an endless well of colorful textured language from the realm of the Great Mystery and the depths of our heart and soul. Each sacred offering is a clue to the truth of who we are, leading us closer to ourselves and why we're here at this time. It's an opportunity for us to take an individual journey into our inner landscapes, bringing forth our deepest expression and the embodied truth felt deep in our bones. This is why I love to weave expressive arts into all of my immersion experiences. I innately know, sense, and feel that every creation is inscribed with the mark of the Creator, including each and every one of us. Creativity is also as essential as the air we breathe; bringing forth our own unique expression is our life blood.

I deeply believe that we are all artists and creators, co-creating each day in service to the Great Cosmic Masterpiece and this dance of life in which we're all a part. The life we are living in this very moment is the true work of Sacred Art. And if we infuse them with deep meaning, and focus our energies on what matters most for the greater good and next seven generations, then our lives become works of he(art), too. It's doing all you can to unleash your authentic soul expression so you can Sparkle SHAMELESSLY® in service to all those who need you most, and to Life itself.

The images that speak to me are universal, tapping into the nature of the cosmos and all that is, relating to our intimate connectedness with others and the great Web of All Life, and reminding us of who we are and to whom we belong. They are archetypal and revelatory, prophetic and liminal, like direct scribes from the soul.

For many years I have had deep connection and communion with all the symbols included on the cover of the book since they originate from my ancestral heritage and diverse spiritual lineages: the Celtic Triquetra symbol of the power of 3, the animal medicine of the hummingbird and the bee with honey, the Mayan temple, and of course, Grandmother Moon. So many of our bodies on this earth are inextricably connected to the pull of the moon, regardless of how we identify out in the world. It's like the person is sipping on stardust and being directly bathed by the silvery liquid light of the moon.

PHOTO BY JONATHAN GRASSI

Words can't do this he(art)work justice, however. In truth, there is a much greater richness to the image if you just sit with it and allow the Great Mystery to unfold before you as a guide to its deeper wisdom. May it be a blessing and a visual prayer that helps us to connect even deeper to our own sacred body wisdom.

Find out more about Lainie Love Dalby or commission your own Shamanic Healing he(art)work at **www.lainielovedalby.com** or on Instagram @LainieLoveDalby.

CONTENTS

Liberating Our True Self from the Bondage of Outdated Belief Systems

BY JANE ASHLEY, *PUBLISHER*

"As a woman, I had always struggled with my body—and I see now how deeply this affected my happiness and kept me from being present and fully embracing my life and potential. As a Publisher, the need for this conversation is obvious, since body image and self love strike so deeply in our collective soul. It's time to uncover and alchemize the shame we carry and the guilt we feel, and offer the voices of transformation—embodied leaders and healers who share their wisdom and guidance to help others meet this dark energy and bring light to their path forward."

~JANE ASHLEY

In the United States, we live in a culture dominated by patriarchal systems of oppression, a capitalist fervor to consume, and by endless collective beliefs that assault our bodies with judgment. These damaging thoughts and behaviors are dictated by the matrices of the dieting industry, the clothing industry, the beauty industry, the pharmaceutical industry, the educational system, and so on.

Women's bodies are products of and at the mercy of this maelstrom of misogyny—and it's up to each one of us to break free of these beliefs and remember that our body is a Divine Home in which our Soul resides.

The big lie? As a female, you are broken and there is something that needs to be fixed.

Stepping onto the path of embodiment results in healing this uninvited belief of brokenness, because once we truly embrace our bodies and remember our inherent wholeness, we discover our Truth: in my case, that love is the only thing that is real, and we all share this human existence together— as ONE being.

As children, we adopt the beliefs of our parents, religious institutions, friends, and school systems. There are likely many stories, voices, and beliefs that have been standing in the way of your own evolution, and for this, you must discern which of them are true—and which of them are lies. Then, you can create a *new* inner dialogue with your highest self in the driver's seat, which gives you the freedom to make new choices unencumbered by outdated beliefs. Now you can own your worth, sovereignty, power, and magic.

The key to fully reprogramming your internal thought loops and evolving past old belief systems is to transmute their energy with truth and the vibration of love. Walking the path of love is a commitment! It's a life-long process of evolution, with no finish line. Living this way gives us the tools to be more intimate with each other and be at peace.

The idea for this collaborative book, *Sacred Body Wisdom,* came to me last year while, in a yoga class, I was holding a downward facing dog pose. Even though I'd been practicing yoga for years, I'd fallen off the horse when my husband and I became full-time caregivers for his elderly mother. Three years later, I'd finally found my way back to the mat, and in that moment in downward dog, suddenly my awareness blew open and I remembered. I remembered the crystalline structure of my bones. I remembered my body as a receiver and transmitter of energy. I felt energy flowing in and out of different meridians in my body. I felt a deep drop down, as if my Soul had "fallen" into every cell of my body. It was a quantum leap into presence. I was being held by the Divine.

And so, finally, after years of going to therapist after therapist trying to figure out why I loathed my body SO much, yoga had shown me what was inside of me all along—the gift of Sacred Body Wisdom.

Now, I accept my body as my sacred vessel. I love myself unconditionally, just as I love my own daughters. I feel my feelings without running away from uncomfortable moments. Instead, I stay present, feel it all, and then release it without getting stuck in story. Within minutes, I've transmuted all self-sabotage, self-criticism, judgment, fear, anxiety, and density...back into love...power...confidence.

Now that I am in a conversation with my body, I feel Life pulsing through me. I feel the blood running through my veins. I am ALIVE with kundalini energy traveling up and down my spine. My chakras are spinning and glowing. I hold EVERY part of my body with reverence and sacredness. I practice gratitude for life. And I forgive myself for any past self-abuse.

Every author in this book has stepped up to their edge, and boldly and vulnerably shared their TRUTH about Sacred Body Wisdom and how they've brought that knowledge forward as part of their soul's work in the world. You'll read real stories about overcoming illness and being rebirthed into a new relationship with the body. You'll read about powerful processes for educating and fostering inclusivity inside of traditionally white dance spaces. You'll read about transforming loneliness and despair into the light of integrated wholeness and embodied self-love. You'll feel inspired to change, too.

However you choose to read and integrate the wonderful wisdom from these authors, I honor your willingness to open up and trust that your body has all the answers to your questions. All that's required is a willingness to love yourself and listen to the highest voice inside your heart. Then, your Soul and your body can partner to create the most amazing life, where ALL parts of your experience—light and shadow—are sacred.

Shakti Healing:
Finding My Way Home to BodyLove

BY RIMA BONARIO

Up until a few years ago I had no idea what people meant when they talked about body wisdom. Seriously. For me, when it came to my spiritual journey, my body was at best an afterthought, at worst an impediment. The truth was, for most of my life my body was not my friend.

Like many people in my generation, my parents would with some regularity discipline me with spankings, whippings with belts and shoes, slaps, arms squeezes, and the like. There were a couple stand-out moments of outright abuse. I felt betrayed by my body and the pain it felt. So, like many children who were disciplined in such a way, I developed the habit of leaving my body to avoid feeling the pain or the shame. This became my go-to coping mechanism, even without any conscious decision to make it so. Studies show that when a coping strategy chosen by your body (fight/flight/freeze) works in a moment of trauma, the nervous system is much more likely to choose that same strategy over and over until it becomes a habit. Leaving my body was a viable way out for me.

It seemed my body continued to betray me. For example, I would randomly wet the bed from ages three through twelve. The last time I can recall it happening, I was so ashamed that I took all my sheets to the basement and tried to wash them by hand in the sink. Then I tried to scrub the mattress to make the wet stain go away—but, of course, there were years of stains on that mattress marking my shame in layers of light-brown rings.

I couldn't imagine facing my parents with a wet bed again, so I decided to run away. I left home around 6:30 a.m. on my bicycle that summer morning in shorts and a t-shirt but I didn't get very far. A block and a half down, a huge dog chased after me and cornered me, barking and barking in my face as I cried in terror. I headed back home to face the monster I knew rather than the monsters I didn't. I had locked myself out as I was determined not to return. So, with my shame complete, I hid under the back porch shivering in the morning cold until, some two hours later, I heard my mom open the back door. When the coast was clear, I snuck inside and never told anyone what happened. I continued to have bladder control issues and even once peed my pants at the bus stop in front of the boy I liked when I just couldn't hold it any longer. I was in eighth grade.

My issues with my body seemed to accelerate after that. We were not an active or sporty family, and even though I loved dance and joined a dance class that year, my body would once again betray me, this time through no fault of its own. One night, my father inadvertently killed my love of dance by announcing while watching Debbie Reynolds dancing on TV that she was just not a good dancer because you had to have long legs to be a good dancer—something she didn't have, and at 5 foot 1 inch, neither did I. I quit my dance class a couple of weeks later. That probably seems nuts to you, but to me it was just common sense. Why waste my Saturdays doing something I could never be good at?

As I moved further into my teen years I was in for my biggest body betrayal—puberty. Having grown up in an Italian Catholic family, my faith had taught me that bodies were sinful and could get me into deep trouble. I found myself at war with my growing attraction to boys. I was told that even my thoughts would require confessing. The message was clear—my desires were unclean. My monthly bleeding was just a marker of this potential doom. My hips filled out and my butt bubbled. In the pre-Kardashian days, this was not good. I earned the nickname *Beach Ball Behind* from my cousins the summer just before I turned fourteen.

The absolute final straw came in sophomore year of high school, when my breasts finally decided to make an appearance. Really, I should say my breast and a half—or at least that's how I saw it. One of my breasts was quite a bit smaller than the other and, to me, it looked hideous. This was not how it was supposed to be, according to all the magazines. Holy cow, what a mess! I seriously hated my body.

The one saving grace was I had been raised to value my mind above all else. Being smart and able to figure things out was all that was recognized as valuable in my family. There wasn't the usual pressure to be beautiful or appear any particular way. It was all about the brains. So, I cut myself off from my traitorous body and focused on my studies. In many ways, that worked for me. I just made peace with the fact that I was smart rather than attractive. I learned how to get approval by producing good work and being a solid team player. My life became all about achievement—something that eventually became completely unsustainable.

In my twenties, I got married and was divorced three years later. That painful experience led me to question my Catholic upbringing, providing the catalyst that launched me onto another, more loving spiritual path; a spiritual path that taught me the value of my heart.

The heart awakening I had was one of the coolest moments of my life. I was reading Don Miguel Ruiz's book *The Mastery of Love: A Practical Guide to the Art of Relationship* (which I highly recommend) and just about four pages from the end I had a thought about what I was reading and my heart just blew wide open. Tears of love and joy ran unchecked down my face as I looked around and suddenly could *see and feel* how I was one with everything and everything was one with me. I looked outside my apartment window and saw the swaying trees and thought, "Wow, that's me!" I saw the roses on my coffee table and, putting a petal to my forehead, I felt oneness with it. I laid on my floor for a long time reveling in the waves of love that seemed to be at once pouring into me and emanating from me. I literally was LOVE.

This awakening lasted for five full days. Whether I was at work, running errands, or visiting with friends, I found myself feeling completely connected to everyone and everything. When I would see someone different than me because they had a mohawk or baggy pants or drove a Hummer (back then, I thought people who drove Hummers were killing the planet), rather than having a separation or judgmental thought, I said, "Oh look! I get to have a mohawk...or wear baggy pants...or drive a Hummer!" Unfortunately, on the fifth day I wondered how long it would last, and within two hours it had faded. Even so, the experience was so very inspiring and radically changed my life. I became committed to having that sense of oneness be my everyday experience.

The irony isn't lost on me that it took me finding the wisdom and holy nature of my body to be able to make that goal a reality.

Shortly after that experience, I found a new love and married again. I also dove headlong into serious spiritual study. At this point, my spiritual study became about moving up and away from my human nature and seeking to connect more deeply to my divine nature, stepping away from Rima as an individual and connecting more with the ubiquitous nature of the ONE.

My studies eventually led me to pursue a doctorate in Transformational Psychology with an eye toward helping myself and others heal unresolved childhood wounds. My program was an amazing blend of science and spirituality. And it was in that program that I came face to face with the biggest block to my continued spiritual development—an unresolved wound of the biggest kind: I still hated my body.

In my course work I was introduced to the idea that my body was intelligent—and it had so much information to offer me—maybe even more than my mind or even my heart. I learned of the vast amount of information that could be gleaned through connecting with and listening to my body. This was a revelation. I was so used to ignoring my body, I had absolutely no clue how to hear it. I routinely worked for six hours straight without food or water, or even getting up. I could power though nights of minimal sleep to study for tests or complete assignments. I was a master at keeping even my basic needs, not to mention my deepest desires, hidden from myself. This kind of drive allowed me to run three somewhat successful businesses, but this could not continue.

As I approached mid-life, my disconnection from my body and my inability to own, let alone articulate, my needs was taking its toll. I found myself feeling so exhausted from building my business, taking care of my family, taking care of my home, and trying to take care of myself, that being intimate with my beloved husband became just one more thing on my to-do list. Just another chore. I deeply loved my husband, but we just couldn't connect very well in the bedroom.

Like so many women, I had been giving so much of myself. *We give so much of ourselves*—to our children, our parents, our communities, our careers. It's no wonder that it feels like we are giving out!

I was lucky. My doctoral program had led me to the realization that if I was going to be successful in my mission to help myself and others heal from childhood wounds, I had to commit to being here fully, on the planet, *in my body.*

I needed to become an embodied woman.

Being in my body was still uncomfortable for me. Years of nervous system adaptations and low-grade anxiety kept it constantly on edge. It was my "normal." I needed to find a new way to be in order to stay present in my body, but ignorance about my body's energetic anatomy was in the way. I had no idea that my body was first and foremost an energy field. And I had no idea how to properly manage and maintain my energy for optimal functioning. Most of us do not know how to do this. And it's so important because the modern era has us under stress like never before—in a constant state of high alert with the speed of life. We are usually over amped or under amped.

This was interfering with my ability to show up in the state of LOVE I had experienced years before. I have come to call this state BLISS or PRESENCE. And I have learned that it happens most often when I am embodied, in my power, and when my heart is open.

There were two things I learned that helped me make this shift:

1) THE IMPORTANCE OF RECEIVING

I am not sure if I ever understood the importance of receiving or if I just shut it all down when my desire to receive sexually came on line. There are so many ways we can receive: energetically, spiritually, and physically. In my years of working with women on making this shift, I have seen over and over that receiving is hard for most of us. We have hearts made for giving. We love to give. We give to demonstrate our love. And it can be hard to let others do things for us.

Women love to give, but we are also made to receive. And when we balance the two, we can tap into a wellspring of feminine energy that resides in our body. Some people call this energy *Shakti* (the Sanskrit word for Life-Force Energy). I call it my *feminine super-power*.

Tapping into my Shakti has changed everything for me. I invested significant time and money to study with masters of energy and Tantric practices, and I began the deep healing work of coming home to my body, mind, heart, and soul. I came to understand that Shakti Life Force Energy is my birthright, and as I learned how to let it flow in and through me, miraculous things began to happen.

2) THE IMPORTANCE OF ENERGETIC MASTERY

In all my years of study, one of my most profound discoveries was coming to understand how to master my own energy field. Now that my Shakti was flowing, I needed to know how to direct it. These are the three most useful tools I learned to support me in this:

GROUNDING—This is the practice of keeping myself energetically connected with the earth. Quantum science has shown us that the most accurate way to describe physical reality is a series of overlapping energy fields. The earth, and every living thing on it has an energy field, including us. We are constantly exchanging energy with everything around us. One of the most import energy exchanges we can make is with the earth. We are designed to give and receive energy from the earth—and this is especially useful when we have too much or not enough energy in our system. Every electrical system we create has a "ground" to keep it from short circuiting if it gets overloaded. And, we can draw energy up from the earth into our bodies, so we don't have to expend the energy in our organs and tissue to live a vibrant life.

CORE—This is the practice of connecting with our energetic center. Often in spiritual circles you will hear people talk about being centered, meaning not getting upset. That is certainly one aspect of being in our core. Yet it goes deeper. *If we are in our core, we are connected to our power.* It is much easier to stay out of upset no matter what is happening if we feel empowered in that situation. The lie most of us have been sold is that we need something outside of us, some external circumstance, someone else's behavior, to change in order for us to relieve our upset. This is a losing proposition that leaves us at the mercy of people and things we cannot control. We become victims. Standing firmly in our core shifts that completely.

EDGE—Every electromagnetic energy field has an edge. The earth's edge is the atmosphere, and that edge protects us from all manner of space junk. We also have an edge—and it's intelligent and programmable. I had no idea about this. I used to get irritated when my husband would come home from work and his "grumpy" mood would invade my space and sully my peaceful state of mind. Come to find out, my edge was almost non-existent, so my field permeated the entire house. No matter where the poor guy stepped in the house he couldn't help but annoy me. I had left no room for him, energetically. Unbeknownst to me I had terrible energetic hygiene. I learned how to work with my edge to help it become strong and thick, to keep my energy in closer to my body (about 2 to 3 feet). This not only created breathing room for my husband and daughter, which they sorely needed, but allowed me to retain more of my energy for myself, alleviating much of my exhaustion. Further, it allowed me to more skillfully keep any negative or cloudy energies out of my space. This was life-changing for me.

Putting these three tools together, I feel as strong and unshakable as a giant oak tree, rooted firmly in the earth (grounded), with a tall and solid trunk (core) and a protective bark (edge).

Together with the practice of finding and unleashing my feminine life force energy or *Shakti*, my relationship with my body has completely transformed. Beyond my wildest imaginings I have come to love my body, not in spite of its uniqueness but because of it.

I am in my fifties now and I feel sexier than I ever have. And as you might guess, that's making my intimate life much more exciting and fulfilling. Being an embodied woman has become a way of life for me. And it gives me enormous pleasure to support other women in finding their way home to themselves.

It's time to wake up lovely.
It's time to remember.

We are being called home.
And we are ready to remember.

To remember the vision that you are.
You are The Divine come to walk upon the Earth.
To restore Peace, To embody Life.

You are beautiful—
A burning fire.
A luscious body.
A powerhouse of love.

You are whole and holy.
Now and forever.
The time has come to be seen.
We are ready. You are ready.

Be bold. Be free. Be wild. Be YOU!

Find your sisters and join hands.
For today we wake,
Together.

Dr. Rima Bonario is a dream weaver, soul coach, and wild heart healer. Her life's work is facilitating and teaching processes and practices that bring about a re-connection to our inherent, sacred wholeness.

Rima speaks and teaches on women's sovereignty and awakening. She offers in-person and online workshops, group and private coaching programs, as well as through hands-on healing sessions. She weaves together elements of modern science and ancient wisdom, myth and archetype, ritual and ceremony, and Soul/shadow work.

Rima's most recent offerings include body-based energy practices and explorations in the arenas of sexual sovereignty and embodied feminine presence.

Rima holds a doctorate in Transformational Psychology and has studied with Soul Mentor Sera Beak, Master Energy Teacher Lynda Caesara, Toaist Healing Master Mantak Chia, and Master Tantric Educators Tj Bartel and Charles Muir. She resides in Las Vegas, Nevada with her husband Tobias and her daughter Sophia. Learn more about Rima and her work at **rimabonario.com.**

Special Gift

7 DAYS TO AWAKEN—LIVE LIFE LUSCIOUSLY!

Get up close and personal with your body. In just 5-7 minutes per day, learn a new and potent body-based technique for tapping into your uniquely feminine life-force energy. Each day will help you connect with and appreciate different aspects of your body to awaken the juiciest, most creative and vibrant parts of yourself—in just seven days!

Get access here: **7daystoawaken.com**

Transforming the Culture of Whiteness in Dance and Sexuality Communities

BY ZAHAVA GRISS (Z)

HOW INCLUSIVITY MIGHT LOOK IN BODY-CENTERED COMMUNITIES

Imagine you enter a round dance studio in the woods. The sunlight and trees are visible through the enormous windows. 130 people are sitting around the edges of the room, ripe with excitement for the week-long festival ahead of us. You look around and notice that there is no racial majority. There are people of Asian, African, Latin, European, and Native American heritage all gathered in the same space. People's bodies are all different sizes...large curvy bodies...petite muscular bodies...three people are in wheelchairs. One person has ALS, one has cerebral palsy, one has a spinal cord injury. Each of these bodies is in contact with someone. There's a gentle hand on a shoulder of someone, another soft spine nuzzling into a leg of someone in a wheelchair. Each body, no matter it's ability, race, gender, age or size, is connected to the body next to it with the most natural and easeful contact with a few exceptions of people who have asked to not be touched.

There is Mohican music playing as we enter. Most people in the room know it is Mohican music. We know the Mohicans are the People of the Waters that are Never Still who lived on this land before they were removed westward. There is a spirit of deep appreciation for this land and for the people who lived here before us. Our experience of the land is more present as we listen to the music. We notice the baby skunk family running by out the window. We notice the quiet open sound of the woods. We notice the soft wood floor under our bare feet. We notice how precious it is to be on this land in this moment with each other.

We have come together for a festival exploring intimacy, play, and dance. We have come together to acknowledge the emerging expansion of leadership in the U.S. to better include women, trans people, non-binary people, and people of color. The facilitators who will be guiding us this week are mostly people of color. The few who are white have dismantled whiteness in their own identity and facilitation practice.

We are giddy with excitement as our eyes move across so many loving faces. We are here to PLAY. The people who have been here before are bubbling with joy to reconnect. They are also sharing sweet welcoming gazes to the new eyes in the room. They are grateful to see our community expanding and curious to get to know who is with us this time.

The new people see others in the room who look similar to them. They soften into the kind touch being offered by new friends at their sides. This growing community has come together to practice new ways of building intimacy through dance, kink, and erotic grief rituals to honor our ancestors. We have gathered to create and nourish the partnerships we love. We have gathered to make love through our dances, and to discover new truths about our gender expression. We have gathered to dismantle our beliefs about what relationships are supposed to look like and instead create intentional relationships that honor who we really are.

We have gathered to heal from sexual abuse and past relationships, and to learn from the past. We have come to explore what we LOVE about sex, intimacy, and play! We are here to bring out the joy in each other as we share our desires and receive them. We are here to learn how to voice our intentions, our requests, our hell yes's and our no thank you's. We are here to remind each other that we belong and our truth is a contribution to the community. We are here to explore what a festival of dancers can discover and how we can contribute to the cultural shifts we desire to see in our society around the body, intimacy, and power.

So many parts of the vision I just shared have come from moments that really happened—moments when I noticed, "Oh this is what it feels like to be at a celebration with no racial majority and with so many genres of music and dance! This is what it feels like to co-create the culture of the space together, because there is no 'dominant' culture that becomes the norm. This is what it feels like to focus my attention on people I had not been focusing on. This is the felt sensation that what I'm seeing now is a truth I couldn't see before as I turn my attention from my own experience to the experience of others. This is what I notice when I connect with the land and the life growing here. This is what it's like to be part of a group where some people are familiar and some people are not, but we all want to know more about each other.

I'm guessing that if you're reading a book about Sacred Body Wisdom you may be part of a body centered community or you may want to be. Perhaps it's a community that loves dance, yoga, kink, Sufi Dancemeditation, sensual partner dance, play parties, bodywork, or somatic experiencing. These are some of the body centered communities I engage in.

I wrote this chapter because so many of the body centered events and communities I have explored are mostly white people, white leadership, and white culture. What do I mean by white culture? I mean there are certain ways of communicating, an aesthetic of what is valued and acceptable, an unspoken way of framing what being a body is, what "safety" is, what spirit is, what having a body means, what success or beauty means that is familiar to a dominant white culture. There is an often unconscious culture that has been created by those who came before us that does not acknowledge or reflect awareness and respect for people of color, who make up the majority of people on this beautiful earth. While people are often saying they want a more diverse community they haven't yet created a culture shift that supports racial diversity. In 2018, with our current government people are more ready to acknowledge racism is a problem and curious how to make a difference. I wrote this so we could better observe white culture, envision what we want to replace it with, clarify what diversity means to us personally, and take action to create the society we want to live in.

MY STORY

My parents come from two extremely different cultures. My whole life I've been code switching. My dad is a Jewish New Yorker from a middle class family that came to the U.S. to escape the Pogroms in Russia and Poland. My mom is an Appalachian woman from Kentucky. She's the first one to go to college in her family who came as indentured servants from the debtors prisons and mental asylums of England to work the coal mines. My parents come from different class, cultural, religious, education, and geographic backgrounds. The only thing they seem to have in common is being white. So I got really curious about whiteness.

My dad was a sociologist studying in Uganda and Nigeria as a student at Princeton. They had a budget cut and sent him to study poverty in Appalachia where he met my mom. I'm the baby of a sociologist and the people he was studying.

I live in the gap between white academia and a culture that is invisible to mainstream America. Raising awareness about white culture is so dear to my heart because it starts to bridge this gap that I live in and so many others live in.

From age two, I was in the dance studio learning how to move my body. I grew up in a dance conservatory culture that felt like a bubble. Our focus on ballet wasn't very relevant to the people outside our community. We would make the shows we wanted to make and hope that people who loved us showed up to watch. My dad would often tell me after watching hours of leaps and turns that he didn't understand how we were making a change in the world. I didn't have an answer for him. I knew I loved dance and I knew I wanted to share my love for it in a way that contributed to society.

By age eleven, I was getting paid to perform with the Joffrey Ballet at the Kennedy Center. I seemed to be on a professional track that was rigorous and prestigious. It was exciting to be supported in my love for dance, but we were doing the Nutcracker. We were memorizing and replicating classical movements without any context for what it meant to us. We didn't really learn much about each other in the process. There wasn't any room for improvisation or even much conversation.

One day when I was training with the Princeton Ballet we had a West African dance class. I remember we all had sore necks for days because we weren't used to letting go in our spine like that. I LOVED it and I wanted more. It was the gateway for me to explore African Diasporic Dance. I was incredibly welcomed into dancing with Urban Bush Women, Katherine Dunham, Ron Brown, Tania Isaac, and Wanjiru Kamuyu. As a teenager into my late twenties I was invited to dance in mostly black spaces, to learn their stories, and to perform their stories on stage and on Black Entertainment Television (BET). This gave me perspective on how culture shapes what dance is, what the body is, and what community is.

I was finally around people who could relate to my experience of living between cultures and who understood the gap between white culture and cultures invisible to mainstream America. I was so relieved to no longer feel alone in this gap. Most of my friendships, romances, and collaborations from age eighteen to thirty-four were with people of color while I was living in New York City. I didn't know how to share what I could see with most of my white friends, but I really wanted to.

I started a dance company called White Folks Soul, By Any Dance Necessary with three incredible white women who were all doing undoing racism work. We had been working with the People's Institute for Survival and Beyond which offered undoing racism workshops. They were really powerful for raising awareness of privilege but they were sitting and talking. We started to partner with them to bring dance into the process. We asked people to dance what breaks their heart and what heals their heart about race. We got vulnerable, we cried, we shook our bodies, we witnessed each other so deeply.

Our dance company visited each others' families and supported each other to see and understand how our parents and our upbringing socialized us to be white. My friendships with these three women became some of my closest relationships and gave me a deeper understanding of the intimacy possible when we question white culture. I still remember when Jesse came with me to Kentucky to meet my extended family and see the house my grandfather built on the side of a mountain. I remember the shame I felt when she saw the poverty of my family and the relief that it was no longer my secret that I came from a part of the white American experience most people never know about.

So many of us who are white in the U.S. don't know our family history or connect to the culture of our ancestors. The more I danced the stories of the African Diaspora the more I wanted to know about my own history and the cultures of my lineage. I didn't really know the dances of my people or who I could learn them from. I started to grieve this missing piece that I didn't even know was missing until I experienced the power of dancing with people who did have a strong embodied cultural lineage.

As I danced with the African Diaspora we were dancing the stories of slavery, the fertility dances to call in new life, the harvest dances to celebrate the earth. These dances connected me to human life in a way that the Nutcracker never did. These dances gave me a way to say thank you to life and a way to be in community. The drummers gave us rhythms that moved us so deeply into a sweat and then eased us into the wisdom of the body that would take over right when I felt too exhausted to keep dancing. My love for life and the power of the rhythm and the connection with the drummers would carry me into a surrendered place. My spine became fluid, my pelvis opened, my eyes brightened, my feet felt so alive on the Earth, my mind was easy and my heart was bursting. My dance community was cheering me on celebrating my soul. It nourished me so deeply and it made me realize how much we were missing this in ballet, in modern dance, in yoga, in white movement spaces. I thought if dance can perpetuate white culture then it can also transform white culture. I started to teach dance for the purpose of replacing white culture with a culture of inclusivity and wholeness.

Today I'm a dancer, kink educator, and coach. I am the director of *Do Good Things with Power*, a leadership immersion for people transforming our culture around intimacy and power. Most of my clients are dance teachers, yoga teachers, sex educators, kink educators, somatic practitioners, sacred sexuality practitioners, bodyworkers, and performing artists. I support them to lead body wisdom spaces that are inclusive, purposeful, erotically intelligent, and conscious of personal and systemic power dynamics.

My professional training came from certifications in Yoga for Two (prenatal, postnatal, and labor coaching), Pilates, Esalen Massage, Deep Bodywork, Urban Tantra, Coaching from the Academy of Coaching Excellence, 35 years of dance training, and many more teachers who do not live within the realm of certifications and regulated education.

I teach dance, trauma release, and how to access pleasure to anti-racist activists to build their resilience and vitality. I teach sensual yoga and erotic presence practices to cancer survivors and sexual abuse survivors so they can reconnect with their erotic power and have meaningful intimacy. I teach dance communities who want to explore eros how to discover and communicate their erotic desires, gender expression, and power exchanges so they can have more fun and ease creating the relationships they desire. I teach sensual birth dances at midwifery conferences so midwives can support moms to give birth owning their erotic energy as part of their power. I teach entrepreneurs creating social change how to access their passion, vulnerability, and presence through the body so they can lead ventures from their heart.

I collaborated with Deepak Chopra to cross pollinate meditators and activists so we can bridge our personal and social wellness. I teach Naked Yoga so yogis can connect with sensuality and pleasure. I teach Erotic Yoga for Kinky People to acknowledge and consciously play with the power dynamics of the teacher student relationship and to nourish the health of our kink communities.

For fifteen years I guided women to explore the alchemy of sex and spirit through dance so we could have a sense of belonging and ecstasy in our body and our relationships. Then my gender identity expanded beyond woman to gender transcendent and I wrote a chapter in *Queer Magic: Power Beyond Boundaries*. I support many clients who are gender non conforming, trans, kinky, poly, or redesigning their expression of their gender, sexuality, and relationship lifestyle. I teach workshops on race, gender, power exchange, and how to touch your sexy self so we can have more fun and ease loving each other! These are the ways I have found to make dance relevant and to contribute to the society I want to live in.

WHITE CULTURE AND SACRED BODY WISDOM

What does race have to do with sacred body wisdom? Here are some questions to consider:

1. When you think about sacred body wisdom, what image comes to mind?
2. Whose body do you think of?
3. When you remember the last yoga class or dance class or play party you attended, who was guiding it?
4. When you studied health in middle school and high school, were the images in the textbook of white bodies?
5. When you grew up going to health class was your teacher white? Have most of your doctors, dentists, gynecologists (if you have one) been white?

I don't know what your answers are.

However, I do know that many of the people who guided my relationship with my body wisdom as teachers, health care practitioners, and medical models have been white. I also noticed that I hadn't noticed that until I entered a black dance community in high school. The more I started dancing in the African Diasporic dance communities and then later in Senegal the more I noticed how unusually white many body-centered communities are in the U.S.

What is "white culture?" Someone's ethnicity, ancestry, country of origin are all distinctly different than someone's race. Race was invented in the mid 1600s by the elite class in early America in order to divide and conquer the working class so they would not unite around their shared interests. In the beginning white did not include Jews, Irish, or Italians. But over time "white privilege" was extended to these groups to protect against people of color becoming a majority and challenging the systemic power of the ruling class.

The invention of race was designed to interrupt our relationships and segregate people with different experiences. Today many well intentioned anti-racists are pointing to the problem or calling people out in a way that continues to divide us. Race was designed to create division and until we learn how to build relationships and move forward together as a team, racism is still creating the result it was intended to create. Transforming racism and white culture is a call for us to come back into authentic relationship with each other which includes acknowledging our history.

White culture has impacted all of us in the U.S. I'm not just talking about white people, I'm talking about people of any race who may be living white culture consciously or not. Simply by living in this country created by colonization we are not immune to white culture. No matter how loving we are and how much we might value inclusivity it might be hard to shift white culture until we can observe it. Let's look and see some ways it may show up.

HOW WHITE CULTURE SHOWS UP IN BALLET

I was socialized as a white girl in the U.S. so when I wanted to dance, my family sent me to ballet. From age 2-20, ballet training was central to my life. I'm incredibly grateful for the way ballet gave me a chance to fly, to feel my strength, to express my grace...I had *so* much energy, ballet gave me a place to harness and direct that energy. It also taught me many things that challenged my humanity—things that are normal occurrences in white culture.

During my "bunhead recovery" I learned that many people recovering from being in the military have had a similar healing process. Whether or not you experienced ballet, some of these may be familiar to you:

1. Your value comes from your ability to follow directions and to look "beautiful."
2. Your beauty and value is defined by being in a skinny, tall, muscular, symmetrical able body, with traditional gender presentation. It's normal for most girls to have anorexia and bulimia given the current standards for weight. I lost my menstrual cycle and fertility due to low body fat when I was training twelve hours a day at the Juilliard School. This is common for ballet dancers and athletes.
3. You are here to perform the director's vision. Your value is determined by your ability to train your body and to be the instrument of the director (or your boss). Your own expression is not valued. In my choreography class at Sarah Lawrence College I asked one of the dancers in my piece if she wanted to show a solo we were working on. The piece was about

racism on campus. My dancer was Dominican and the solo was created to explore an emotionally courageous and vulnerable state. I wanted to empower the dancer to choose if this was the moment to share it with the mostly white class. My teacher was white and turned to me and told me, "Don't ask your dancer, tell your dancer what to show."

4. The teacher or director will control how you move, what you wear, and where you put your attention. There is no negotiation or consent process around this power dynamic. It is assumed that you are a *yes* to this hierarchical dynamic simply by being in class.

5. Your value is based on how you compare to others. This is a competition for who can be the best.

6. It is normal to have a class with all white students, a white teacher, and to dance to music composed by (mostly dead male) white people without acknowledging that this is a white space. It is normal to not notice or speak about who is not in the room. This leads to us not noticing or caring about the impact we have on the people who are not in the room with us.

7. While many other cultures dance for healing, for fertility, to connect with the land, to release grief, or to honor ancestors, it is normal for white dancers to make dance performances that have no relationship to our healing, land, ancestors, or current society. I trained at one of the most prestigious dance conservatories in the U.S., Tisch School of the Arts at NYU. My choreography teacher actually told me "Some topics are too controversial to make dances about" when I made a piece about how many dancers were smokers and how the cigarette industries were targeting ballet dancers who hated themselves for being overweight. Beauty and physical virtuosity were celebrated over dances that raised questions about our culture and status quo.

8. It's more important to move and control your body than it is to feel and heal your body. The mind-body relationship parallels a non consensual master-slave relationship. The mind tends to notice the body to the extent that the body is an obstacle, when it is injured or tight or sick, rather than appreciating how much the body serves us and gives us life!

9. White culture teaches us to be afraid of our sexual power. Our erotic appetite could get us into danger or distract us from having a successful life. In early America black people were hypersexualized and fetishized without consent (like the legendary Sarah Baartman "Hottentot Venus.")

On the flip side, white people were desexualized and repressed. A white woman who expressed her erotic desires was often pathologized as having sexual hysteria. Many movement forms including ballet, yoga, and modern dance in the U.S. hide our erotic nature as if sharing it would delegitimize our artistry. I learned clear messages that sexuality should not be part of my dances if I wanted to have a professional career. One of the most talented dancers at our ballet school growing up made it into Juilliard. Shortly after, I heard rumors that she was a drop out and had to become a stripper and she blew her opportunity to "make it." When one of the dance companies I danced for saw my website with sexual empowerment workshops, they disapproved. Many people assumed I was doing sex work and assumed that sex work was something to be ashamed of and could jeopardize my reputation in the professional dance world.

10. If your dance partners touch your pelvic floor or your breasts you should pretend it didn't happen. If you acknowledge that it happened and speak a boundary you could "cause trouble." I was the only one who spoke up in high school when the men in our pas de deux class touched several of the women. White culture teaches us to not speak about sexuality and that following the directions of the teacher was more important than rocking the boat by speaking up.

Do any of these sound familiar to you? Perhaps you can think of even more that I haven't mentioned.

HOW WHITE CULTURE SHOWS UP IN SEXUALITY

As a kink educator, play party facilitator, bodyworker, and intimacy coach here are some of the ways I have noticed white culture in sexuality:

1. A lot of tantra teachers do not reference that tantra started as a sociopolitical movement that rejected the caste system in India. Tantra highlighted the power inside us rather than the status assigned to us by our society. This aspect of tantra is still relevant to our society today.
2. Many tantra teachers in the U.S. often do not speak about their own racial identity and how it may impact who's in the room and the way they teach.
3. Many "certified" sexuality programs are lead by white people. When I was offering sexual empowerment for anti-racists in the Bay Area, a woman

of color told me she could not find a certified training that was run by people of color. Many indigenous practices around sexual empowerment are not recognized yet in our society.

4. Many workshops that teach consent do not point out that consent is cultural. Different cultures have different ways of relating to consent and expressing affection. There is no one right way to do consent.

5. It's normal at a play party for people to share what they would like to get rather than what they would like to contribute to someone. In white culture there is often a focus on pleasure for yourself rather than the pleasure that comes from being generous. I'm not talking about who is giving or receiving touch because you can be in either one of those roles and the pleasure can still be about you. I'm talking about a culture that values generosity and shows up to a play party to be part of a community and contribute to the people you love.

6. White culture focuses on individual gain. At many play parties people consider their personal fantasy. But imagine what becomes possible if we start a party by asking people to share a fantasy for the community! Many people lose attention for the group when their body becomes aroused. In white culture it's normal or even expected that arousal leads to forgetting our impact on others. One of the things I noticed dancing in Dakar, Senegal with the Wolof people was how much the community celebrated the partnerships in it. There was an understanding that partners contribute to community and community supports partnership. We are interconnected no matter how much arousal is present.

7. We are in the #MeToo era where many consent violations are being brought forward. White culture gives people with social rank a sense of entitlement that they can take what they want without consequences. There are many people who have been leaders or in a role of social rank who are only now being held accountable for a history of violating consent.

8. People assume that someone "in power" or in a dominant role cannot be trusted given our history of nonconsensual power dynamics. My definition of kink is "sexual desires, behaviors, and identities that challenge social approval giving you the opportunity to explore your courage, shame, pleasure, and freedom." Conscious kink is an alternative to this history of mistrust and yet most people do not understand kink or are afraid of it. The most popular movie about kink is *50 Shades of Grey* which does not show a healthy power dynamic. Kink gives us the oppor-

tunity to replace non consensual hierarchy with healthy power dynamics where the leader (or the Dominant) is trustworthy, compassionate, accountable, and committed to the wellbeing of the follower (or the submissive.) The Dominant companions the submissive through their fears with love while affirming a sense of belonging so the sub can crack through shame. White culture cannot see this opportunity for doing good things with power as a Dominant. It does not see the possibility to replace non consensual power dynamics with choice, creativity, intimacy, and shame resilience. Many people who naturally are dominant sexually are afraid to express it or do not learn how to express dominance wisely and constructively.

9. People assume that someone who is sexually submissive must not be powerful. However, surrender is a courageous demonstration that we can trust and be powerful even when we are not in control, which challenges white culture. In conscious kink a submissive cultivates the skills to be responsive, in full choice, self aware, and enlivened by serving others. A submissive masters the ability to transmute intensity into healing and erotic energy. In white culture a submissive is seen as weak. In an effort to appear strong and independent, many people are afraid to be vulnerable and surrender to someone, thus never exploring this part of their sexuality.

YOUR BODY ON WHITE CULTURE

White culture teaches us that your power does not come from how you contribute to others but how you control others. People often freak out when they feel they are losing control. But the body is not something we can control. The body will age, die, sleep, and heal on its own time. We cannot control what our menstruation or birth or miscarriage will look like. We cannot control our height, our metabolism, our skin color, what turns us on, or which genitals we have (without surgery).

We *can* choose whether or not we accept the truth about our body. We *can* increase our capacity to be present with our body. We *can* shift from *controlling* our body to *contributing* to our body. In these ways, we are transforming the way white culture limits our sacred body wisdom. We are softening and disarmoring to become whole and receptive to our aliveness.

WHAT'S POSSIBLE BEYOND WHITE CULTURE?

White people are a minority in the world and are predicted to be a minority in the U.S. around 2040. Whiteness and humanity are incompatible and we are the ones who have the opportunity to support this transition of leadership to happen in a way that honors our history and restores our wholeness.

In this moment in 2018, as I write this so many embodiment spaces, dance classes, sexuality workshops, and body centered education programs are led by people who have not yet deconstructed white culture for themselves or the spaces they lead. I'm not just talking about white people. Anyone living in a society where white culture is prevalent has likely internalized parts of this thinking. This isn't just about continuing the existing culture of our communities with more colorful faces in the room. This is about transforming white culture, replacing it with a new culture, and supporting each other as a team to live this new culture.

The good news is that we don't have to come up with the answers by ourselves. So many other cultures have wisdom we can learn from around the body, dance, sexuality, nature, and living in community. Many yoga and dance classes frame our relationship with our body as what happens within our own skin. But shifting our relationship with our body is about shifting our culture around us and how we interact with each other! It's connected to our ability to observe white culture so we can replace it. It may be harder for white people to see white culture without exposure to other cultures as a point of reference. Many people of color have more opportunities to be in other cultures such that they can see and interrupt white culture more consistently which better serves us all.

The wisdom and inspiration we receive from other cultures is sacred and we can share it without cultural appropriation by focusing on these things:

1. Building a relationship with the people and the culture we are inspired by.
2. Asking for permission and guidance from people in that culture about how to share what moves us.
3. Crediting the source of where something comes from and the context in which it is traditionally practiced.
4. Learning about our own cultural roots even if they are uncomfortable. This may mean grieving that our family no longer remembers who

we come from. Or they remember but they do not see it as a source of belonging or strength. This grief is sacred and essential for us to feel so we are not impulsively using other cultures to numb this discomfort or fill this hole.

HOW DO WE TRANSFORM OUR CULTURE?

I want to share with you one of the most inspiring and successful experiences I've had shifting culture and creating inclusivity in a mostly white, hetero, able-bodied, gender conforming dance community. My desire by sharing this is to inspire you to shift the culture of *your* community. And, it takes time. This specific community is one I first met fifteen years ago.

The way I first started to shift the culture was difficult. I felt angry, isolated, and hopeless. I kept focusing on the ignorance of others. Now years later, I'm having so much more fun and success...and I see how important it was that I didn't give up. Just in case you've questioned staying in the game, this is for you. I'm certainly not sharing this because I have it all figured out, because I don't. I'm sharing this because I'm delighting in my community in a way I didn't know how to in the beginning but longed to. It's such a gift to see this not as a burden but as a way to grow with the people I love. These are the words I wish I could have read fifteen years ago when I first arrived in this community and cried because I couldn't express what it meant to me and it seemed nobody else cared. This is what I learned from being the Diversity Outreach and Support person for a festival called Touch&Play.

I started to observe the thoughts that were getting in my way. Some of it sounded like this:

"They don't care as much as I do. Why don't they understand how important this is? I'm so frustrated I was born as a white person. I shouldn't step into leadership. What can I contribute? I'm white. What if I mess up and the people don't respect me anymore? If I don't get back to the people who gave me critique soon enough they're going to think I don't care and I'm not real. I'm not getting paid enough to do all that it will take. Let's just kick out all the white people in power and start over from scratch. I want to do something but I don't know what to do. It's not going to be enough. I don't think it's really going to change. I tried saying something before and it didn't work. Why would people of color want to come join us anyway?"

Each time these thoughts would come up, my focus would move away from what's important to me and how I want to contribute. As a result, I would get paralyzed and just stop. I realized I can't shift my focus until I see where my focus already is. So I started to observe when I was focusing on all these thoughts I was sick of thinking. As soon as I could see it, I didn't have to *be* it. I could choose to shift my focus to what was most important to me, what my vision is, what I would love to contribute, and what action to take next.

Martin Luther King said, "I have a dream." He didn't say, "I have a problem." Both may have been true, but he demonstrated what it is to see what's possible and to inspire others to see it, too! It's a powerful skill to shift our attention to possibility especially in moments when the here and now isn't working for us. This is a skill I want to nourish in thought leaders like you.

The main question I had to ask myself and ask my community along the way was, "Are you willing to set aside the frustration or resignation around what didn't work in the past in order to focus your attention on what you want to create?" This willingness is what moves us beyond where we have been before and helps us grow.

Our main medicine is our willingness to be inspired by the vision and to be more interested in the vision than in our frustrations.

It's essential to learn how to inspire people to join you in this mindset—not in a way that dismisses their frustrations but in a way that demonstrates compassion and presences what's possible, in a way that gets us excited to create it *together*.

First, clarify your own vision of what you want to see happen. What would success look like and what would it mean to you to have it? Share the possibility you see with other organizers and ask for the time and money you want to enjoy making this vision come true! It's important to feel valued and supported by your team. This work takes several hours each week and the income to support it. So if you're joining a team or creating your own budget, look at what you need to thrive. One of the biggest things I learned is that if I'm underpaid or don't have the time to do this work, I don't show up the way I want to show up.

9 STEPS TO CREATE INCLUSIVITY IN YOUR COMMUNITY

For each of the 9 steps I will share a **principle in bold** and an *example in italics* from our community. The principles are intended to support you as you come up with the unique vision for your community. The examples are to give you inspiration and possibility. It may or may not look like what we created.

1. WHAT'S THE SHARED VISION?

It's so important to create a vision of what success looks like for you and for others in your community, so you can come to a specific shared vision that you all delight in creating together. **Power Loves Precision.** Inclusivity without a specific purpose can lead to a lack of clarity or a weak container.

This is the mission statement our team came up with:

We welcome a diverse community of dancers and somatic visionaries. This is a festival about play, vulnerability, and building community with embodied, emotional, and erotic intelligence. It takes courage, compassion, and consent to play truth or dare with integrity. Sharing one's truth is an act of intimacy. Being daring is about getting outside our comfort zones. If we want something we've never had before, we have to do something we've never done before. This is a space to explore our personal, tribal, and societal desires! What can dance, somatics, tantra, kink, Contact Improvisation, and communication practices contribute to our intimacy? Come ready to cultivate, express, and feel your desires. Let's get compassionate and curious about intimacy, sexuality, consent, emotions, gender, privilege, race, power dynamics, and inclusivity. There's an emerging expansion of leadership in the U.S. to better include women, trans, non gender conforming, and people of color. There's a growing community of people practicing new models of intimacy. We are shifting from an era of sexual abuse to an era of sexual liberation with accountability. What can we, as a festival of dancers, discover and contribute to these cultural shifts?

2. WHAT'S THE GOAL?

Create something specific, measurable, attainable, relevant to the culture shift you desire, and based in time. This makes it something you can work on together in physical reality.

We want our teachers to be 80% poc and nonbinary. We want to only work with white cis teachers who share our vision and values. We want at least 30% of our 140 participants to be people of color, queer, or non gender conforming (ngc) people who are new to our community. We want people returning to our community to see value in expanding our community and to delight in welcoming new people by contributing money and being part of sharing the invitation to new people.

3. WHO'S LEADING TOGETHER?

Our focus was specifically to create more racial and gender inclusivity. So we **built a leadership team that reflected the mission.**

I spent several months researching poc and ngc facilitators who might be a great fit for our festival. I created a database of ninety people by sharing the vision with friends and colleagues and asking for recommendations. I posted on social media. I looked for spaces that I didn't know about yet. I joined facebook groups with poc or ngc intentions and admin to learn about new events and conversations. I attended new poetry and dance performances produced by poc and ngc communities. I looked at the progressive conferences and studios and researched their presenters, wrote to them and shared my vision and asked for recommendations (i.e. Sex Down South, Interfusion Festival, Gibney.) I looked up podcasts by poc and gnc people on sexuality, intimacy, and embodiment.

It's important to see who's already leading this work beyond your normal circles and to listen for who inspires you and then, if the inspiration is mutual, invite them to explore the possibility of collaboration.
This isn't just about finding someone with a specific identity. It's about finding someone who inspires you and who is inspired by you and the opportunity to collaborate. Sometimes that person may be white. What?! **What's most important is to ask them not only how they identify but what their identity means to them and what it means to them to build the specific vision you are inviting them to build with you.**

For us that looked like asking these questions on the teacher application form: "What is your racial identity? How have you explored this identity? How may that impact the way you facilitate and build a mixed race community? What is your gender identity? How have you explored this identity? How may that impact how you teach and build a mixed gender and gender non-conforming community?"

It's important to **be transparent about who the community has included up until now and to ask if they want to be involved and what it would mean to them.** Let them know you want to work with facilitators who would LOVE to be part of this vision. **If it occurs to them as hard work it's likely not going to be fun to collaborate.** If you're clear on what inspires you to work together then when things get uncomfortable (as things tend to do when you try things you've never done before) you can presence what inspires you.

For three years in a row we had poc teachers drop out last minute after signing contracts. I got curious about why this kept happening. The poc teachers who did show up were all my friends and beloveds. They had a relationship to someone in the community. They were enrolled in the shared vision. We also had the budget to cover some of their travel costs. For the future I'd love if we could cover all of it! I also have a desire to be able to offer them a guest ticket to bring a loved one.

Consider how you can demonstrate that you value their presence at the event.

4. MONEY

Money is energy. When I ask people what they really, really want that they aren't sure they can have...it's often something they can't afford. Money is one of the main ways we stop seeing what's possible. Many people may see money as the obstacle to joining the community or to manifesting the vision you hold. **Money can be our ally in our mission by giving people a way to demonstrate who and what they value.** Inviting members of the existing community to contribute financially gives you the chance to connect around the shared vision and to not just wish things were different but to take an authentic action that demonstrates what's important to them. It also communicates a sense of appreciation and welcome for new people entering the community who receive a scholarship.

Create a scholarship fund that aligns with your specific mission.

We created a scholarship fund specifically for dancers who:
- *Are new to Touch&Play and/or new to Earthdance.*
- *Add diversity to our mostly white, hetero, cis-gendered, able-bodied community of American contact improv dancers (by welcoming people of a different race, ethnicity, national origin, gender identity, sexual identity, (dis)ability, or other unique identities we do not know to name.)*
- *Have demonstrated a commitment to exploring building community with embodied, emotional, and erotic intelligence.*
- *Will share their inspiration and wisdom from T&P with your local communities (i.e. educators, practitioners, or facilitators.)*

5. ENROLLING THE COMMUNITY IN THE VISION BEFORE THE EVENT

What is the existing culture of the community? What do you all love to do together? **Engage the community through what it loves!**

We started as a contact improv community that loves to connect through dance. Part of the culture of our community is to create a "score"—an improvisational inquiry or guide. For example, a score could be "falling, how many ways can I fall and bow to the Earth?"

I created the "inclusivity score" to engage the community in a way that was already familiar. The purpose of the inclusivity score was to deepen relationships specifically around the shared value of inclusivity, to presence the new theme (especially for people who had come in the past who may not be tracking this new intention), to share what we are doing differently so far, and to bring our hearts into the conversation.

Engage the community in a heart to heart about what it would mean to them to have more inclusivity in the community.

Each person who called shared from their heart what it meant to me to create more inclusivity in their community. It was important to be specific, vulnerable, and truthful. This was not a theoretical conversation. It was essential to take the time and care to listen to what it meant to each person. For some people, the idea of inclusivity was vague or something that the leaders were doing without them, but this "inclusivity score" made it a personal conversation. It created the quality of attention on inclusivity that we would continue at the event. It demonstrated that we were bringing courage, vulnerability, curiosity, creativity, and compassion to this shift. We weren't making assumptions that we all want the same thing or for the same reason.

In some cases we had people who hadn't thought about it and weren't interested. This was valuable for us to see now rather than to discover at the event later. It gave us the opportunity to have a conversation about what was important to them and why they wanted to be part of the community so we could look and see if it was aligned for them to join us. It was important not to make them wrong for the reasons they wanted to come and to simply clarify what the event is now and ask if they still want to join. What would it mean to them to be part of the vision we have for inclusivity? Asking and listening is more effective than assuming they want to be part of it or telling them why it should be important to them.

Invite them to take specific action that aligns with their desire to create inclusivity. When people see something that's important to them but they don't know what to do next they can experience frustration, cynicism, or resignation.[1] Giving people specific strategic ways to be in action empowers them to demonstrate what's important to them and to be part of a team that shares the same intention and willingness to contribute.

We gave them 3 specific ways to demonstrate what was important to them.

1. *Donate to the scholarship fund to support new people to join our community that would add to our diversity.*
2. *We asked, "Who are some of your friends you would love to invite to our event for the first time who are poc, queer, gnc or would bring diversity in another way? Are you willing to call them to invite them??*

Be present with them as they brainstorm who they love, that they already have a relationship with, that they would love to be of this event. Ask them if they are willing to commit to invite them and by what date. Consider the timing of the invite will be most powerful if it gives invitees enough lead time to explore the opportunity, apply for a scholarship, and share the invite with their circles.

---

[1]   From Academy of Coaching for Excellence

3. *We asked if they would call 4 friends this week from our community to have this conversation with them.*

Focus on inspiring the people who already have friendships to connect with each other around this shared vision for inclusivity. Building a team with people who delight in each other makes it so much more fun. We are a team calling in new people, this is not just about the "leaders" focusing on inclusivity.

I offered to email a list of everyone who had been part of our community the past 2 years to make it easy to think about who to contact and to help us track as a community who had already had the conversation. I also gave them a script for the conversation.

Some people on the list didn't want to come back to the event. Those were some of the most valuable conversations. We asked them what would they want future participants to be aware of. It was important to show that whether or not they attended the next event we valued hearing anything they wanted to share about their experience especially things that would help us see things we could not see before. It can be really powerful and healing to have a friend call and have this conversation who is willing to share anything you want back to the organizing team. In some cases we had sweet cries together and it really deepened our friendship or even had them reconsider coming back.

Belonging to a community is not just about what happens at the event, it's the way we vision together before the event and how we reflect together after the event. It's important for the budget to cover the time you invest before and after the event in this way.

6. OPENING THE EVENT

Voice the vision of inclusivity at the opening circle for the event. By now many people are already connected to the vision and naming it in the space affirms the shared value and sets a tone for people who may be new. Ask yourself if you're willing to be grateful, joyous, and loving as you speak the intention of inclusivity in your community. Your way of being impacts the group more than the words you share.

"I am willing to be grateful, loving, playful, joyous, and creative," I said to myself before I opened the circle with:

"Starting in 1999, I have been in spaces to dismantle oppression. Sometimes as a student, a teacher, a collaborator, an artist, a witness...and I have had moments of struggle, feeling alone, burned out, hopeless, or unable to do enough. I've noticed the magic in spaces that are designed for play, creating art, building relationship, dancing, exploring eros. I've seen how powerful and possible it is to bring our play and creativity to the very things that break our heart. I am weaving a soul family of playmates, a social movement, that has the resilience, the clarity, the ecstasy, the PLAY to transform our lineages and embody love."

Ask people to take a moment to reflect on what creating inclusivity in our community means to us now. It's great to have paired shares or small groups. Create the culture of curiosity, love, courage, and play around this together. Bring awareness to not ask poc or gnc to do the work for us.

For example in our opening circle I said, "We are exploring inclusivity to be more human, more connected, more clear that we belong here. There are many workshops and containers exploring this during the festival. Be mindful that during our 'free time' or unstructured time together we may want to continue exploring. Take a moment to consider if you talk about it with someone will it put one of you in an 'educator role?' If so, ask if they want to have the conversation so it's consensual and something that builds intimacy rather than feeling like 'work.'"

7. VISIBILITY AND BELONGING AT THE EVENT

When people are new to a community how can we support them to feel seen in the way they want to be seen? Not just visible as a new poc or new gnc person, but how can they be visible for who they are, what's important to them, how they want to be welcomed, how they want to contribute? Some people don't like the attention of the whole group and it's more supportive to introduce them to people one on one and share what you love about them. Other people thrive with group attention. Create a way for them to design how they want to be seen like a performance, a story, a panel conversation.

I created a panel to explore inclusivity in our community and featured 5 voices who expanded the group awareness around their specific identities. It was also important to feature voices of people who have a skill set to focus on what's possible rather than only focusing on the problem. This way their voices can be part of the inspiration.

I chose people of different races, genders, and neurodiversity. I also chose people who were both new to our community and familiar. I chose people who were teachers and who were participants so we could bring awareness to these different experiences.

There's often an unspoken social rank that gives more visibility to people based on who's already been here and who's in a leadership position. By choosing people across these spectrums we were intentionally focusing on them because of who they are as a person, and not just their social rank.

Gathering in this way gives the community a chance to practice listening around inclusivity and possibility. It also creates visibility for new people and acknowledges and celebrates the successes we've had so far.

During our panel several new people said they had never felt so welcomed to a community before. It was so energizing for the community to hear this feedback and build on the momentum.

8. WITNESSING TEAM

Create a team of people who are available to support inclusivity. Teachers may or may not have this awareness. The role of this team is to witness the things that have historically been a blind spot in the community so that more people experience being visible. Rather than having poc and gnc people be the ones to point out blind spots in the moment, educate a team to look out and offer support. What do you look for? Ask people who have been and are currently part of the community what they want us to see.

During the "inclusivity score" I compiled a list of many things our poc and gnc wanted us to focus on. This way they don't have to be "on duty" during the event because they have trained us for what to look for in advance. During the training it was important to not make people think they should already know this, but to focus on learning it together now.

Some examples of what our community brought up:

- *You don't know what you don't know. Cultural humility is easier than cultural competency.*
- *Privilege separates us and seeing privilege together can bring us back into relationship.*
- *Anger can be a basis for dismissing someone. If someone is angry or upset it does not mean what they are saying isn't valid. Anger can be a wise and useful response that a boundary was crossed. How anger is expressed can be healthy or unhealthy but it's a wisdom response to a boundary being crossed. Let the person you are supporting know they have a right to feel angry. Be mindful that some people may be socialized to feel scared or vulnerable expressing anger.*

9. WATERS OF THE SOUL: GETTING VULNERABLE AND WET TOGETHER

The body has sacred wisdom. We cannot heal racism with strategy alone. We must grieve together and embody our love for each other. The body knows how to laugh, cry, orgasm. Each of these is a way to tremble, release, and come home to our truth. Laughter, crying, and orgasm are all ways that our involuntary nervous system reorganizes and we let go of whatever our body was holding on to so we can now be more present, more whole, more connected. This trembling deepens our capacity to be present together during discomfort.

Shifting the culture of our community is not an intellectual thing. As my grief teacher Sobonfu Somé would say, "We are here to finish the unfinished business of our ancestors." This is bigger than us. When we are willing to connect with our lineage, we see how we are supported by those who came before us who give us strength and insight. We also see that we are contributors to those who have come before and who will come after.

Sobonfu would tell us that we breathe with the ancestors, just like trees give us oxygen and we give them carbon dioxide. The ancestors give us strength and perspective and we offer them our grief to acknowledge the truth and our willingness to take authentic actions. The ancestors have sacred wisdom but they don't have a body anymore. That's where we come in! **We have bodies to transform emotion and to take aligned action in the physical world in a way the ancestors no longer can.**

The ritual is mostly without words so attention can focus on sharing presence together (not ideas.) We are being present with each other as each person activates their body wisdom to release.

I co-lead an Erotic Grief Ritual with Taina Lyons inspired by Sobonfu's grief rituals of the Dagara Tribe in Burkina Faso. Sobonfu's life intention was to bring this wisdom to the west where she felt it was more needed than back home. She died January 14, 2017. I had the honor of being in ritual with her several times and she asked us to share this and to acknowledge its roots.

When we asked her about cultural appropriation she said, "If you borrow your neighbor's pot to cook dinner, enjoy dinner, and tell everyone at the dinner that you borrowed your neighbor's pot." It gives me tremendous joy to share her magic through these rituals. I hope that you will one day join us. We have expanded beyond the traditional ritual to include eros. When I first started attending Sobonfu's grief rituals I would go to play parties at night and discover that my orgasms were the same deep trembling as my grief at the altar. I shared this with Sobonfu and she smiled and said yes.

Now Sobonfu didn't bring eros into her rituals but I could tell from this moment we shared that she knew what I knew. Later after her death she came to me and guided me to continue this work in a way that connects to our wholeness (including our eros). She told me to call it "Waters of the Soul." This has since become the name of my performance ritual and the erotic grief rituals I lead. I would love to share both of these with you and your community.

This ritual is not just about emotional expression, it is about being a village that loves unconditionally. We are still here with you as you release. The rhythm of the drums and the community singing continues for hours sometimes days. It is about being present with each other in a way that communicates "all is well" even as we tremble with grief or eros.

It is a ritual that acknowledges grief doesn't really happen on the level of the individual, it's collective. It gives us a chance to feel our personal grief, "I feel disconnected and alone," and to see the bigger picture, "I'm grieving the ways racism has disconnected us and interrupted our experience of belonging together on this Earth."

This healing ritual increases our resilience to look, see, tell the truth, and take authentic action that restores our aliveness, our compassion, and ability to live our life's intentions. Our bodies are nature. Our bodies know how to transform grief, pain, disappointment, and loss into connection, presence, and creativity.

WHAT'S NEXT?

My wish is to inspire awareness and what it can look like to transform a white culture into a culture that honors the body, eros, and grief as our allies in being human together. What would you love to contribute to this cultural shift? I offer workshops and coaching to support you to get clear on the contribution you'd love to make, building a team, and staying focused as you take the next small sweet steps. You can learn more about working together at www.EmbodyMoreLove.com.

THANK YOUS

Thank you to the many people who supported me in writing this chapter and who have been my allies over the last 19 years of transforming white culture. Thank you to my fellow organizers of Touch&Play, Alyssa Lynes, Béu Tornaghi, Daniel Hayes, and Moti Zemelman for supporting this inclusivity work and to the whole community that participated in calls, fundraising, showing up at the panel, and having compassionate conversations. Thank you to the Earthdance Diversity Scholarship team. Thank you to Coaching for Social Change and the Academy for Coaching Excellence including Zo Tobi, Mazin Jamal, and Rachel Fryke. Thank you to the People's Institute for Survival and Beyond, Re-Evaluation Counseling, Ruth King, Chelsea Gregory, Sobonfu Somé and to the incredible friends who co-founded our dance company White Folks Soul by Any Dance Necessary, Jesse Phillips-Fein, Alexis Halkovic, and Alyssa Lynes. Thank you Victor Lee Lewis, Anurag Gupta, Teeni Dakini, Nehemoyia Young, Maketa Wilborn, Tamilla Woodard, Will MacAdams and Kaitlin June for co-facilitating spaces to end white supremacy with me over the years. It's an honor and joy to love with you in this way! Thank you Heather Box for supporting me to tell my story in a way that helped me know myself and my role more deeply. Thank you Rha Goddess for being a spiritual guide in my soul work. Thank you to more people than I can name and especially to YOU for reading this.

Zahava Griss (also known as Z, pronouns They/Them) is the founder of Embody More Love providing dance, coaching, kink education, performance ritual and bodywork. Z supports people to express passion for each other and for life! Z has a unique approach to healing race and gender oppression through the body, building meaningful relationships, and demonstrating our shared passions. Z is gender transcendent and a contributing author to *Queer Magic: Power Beyond Boundaries.* Z comes from thirty years of dance training, certifications in Yoga for Birth, Esalen Massage, Urban Tantra Practitioner, Pilates, and Coaching.

PHOTO BY OM RUPANI

Powerful influences include the arts of unlearning racism, Sufi whirling, Sexual Shamanism, bioenergetics, socially conscious entrepreneurship, and transformational group dynamics.

Z directed Spiritual Nourishment for Conscious Activism in collaboration with Deepak Chopra and has been listening to, speaking in, and facilitating spaces to transform white privilege since 1999, including work with the People's Institute for Survival and Beyond, Sarah Lawrence College, the Re-Evaluating Counseling community, and the national White Privilege Conference.

Z currently directs Do Good Things with Power, a leadership immersion for facilitators who are transforming our culture of intimacy. Z has been touring workshops, erotic grief rituals, and dance performances across the U.S. and Europe. Learn more and join the newsletter for upcoming events at **www.EmbodyMoreLove.com.**

Special Gift

This movement sequence activates your presence, clarity, and love. It's a powerful morning practice or ritual before doing something that's really important to you!

Download at: www.embodymorelove.com/embody-more-love-movement-practice/

Coupon to make it free: SACREDBODYWISDOM

Trusting the Current of Body Sensation

BY ROCHELLE SCHIECK

"To embody the transcendent is why we are here."
—SOGYAL RINPOCHE, *THE TIBETAN BOOK OF LIVING AND DYING*

The time has come to remember our essence and embrace the embodiment that makes our human lives possible. There are many maps to help you find your way back to the physical sensation of truth that lives in your bones and breath. The best maps are the ones that work for you. I offer you these words as a way to imagine the sacred marriage between your body and your soul as an experience that is grounding, creative, empowered, flowing with giving and receiving, expressive, intuitive, and culminating with embodied ascension, where we proclaim, "To embody the transcendent is why we are here!"

GROUNDING

We live in tumultuous times. Some refer to this moment in history as *the turning of the ages.* As we participate in and observe the cycles inside and around us, we often ask, how can we stay connected to ourselves, others, nature, and spirit in the midst of so much accelerating change?

One of the most grounding things you can do as our individual and collective reality wobbles is steady yourself in the physical sensation of truth you feel in your body.

When you are connected to your body in the present moment, you have an incredible navigational ability to stay connected to your spirit and be guided through the dance of life's challenges and blessings—based on what you feel in your gut, in your bones and by the goosebumps on your skin.

We already do this—all the time. Sometimes consciously, sometimes unconsciously. Can you recall a moment where your body called you closer to a person or an experience with a magnetic force? Can you also recall a moment when you walked into a room and there was a subtle or strong guidance that directed you away from a person or an experience?

That sensation that lives on top of and below your skin is the sensation of the sacred.

The body is the intermediary between the mind and the soul. The body's wisdom is in its intuitive and instinctive ability to sense truth before the mind can conceptualize it.

For those who feel deeply connected to their body, they enter into more of a flow state with life, trusting the current of sensation as it guides them on their journey.

How does one become more grounded in the sensation of their body? Imagine getting up right now to do something you need or would like to do. Let it be something simple like getting a glass of water. As you rise up or reach down, instead of following the thoughts in your head, follow the feeling in your body. Notice your own ability to drop into the current of sensation that is always available when we bring our attention to it.

This current of sensation grounds you into the truth of the moment by honoring the way that you authentically experience it through the feeling in your body.

CREATION

When rooted into our truth, our bodies and the moment, there is a stronger container to hold and nurture the seed of creation. Most people living at this transformational time have a strong desire to create. Sometimes they are clear on exactly what their project is and other times it is more of an emergent sense that something is coming.

The world is calling for new solutions that are sustainably aligned with nature and the souls of all people. It will not be one individual that leads the way, but millions and billions of people who awaken to their own creative power to co-create with the world around them.

When beginning to follow one's call to create, courage is needed to dream. We must expand our capacity to source our vision from possibility instead of probability, until we remember that what's possible becomes probable when we believe in its potential and offer our lives to nourish its growth.

What is your vision for your own life? For this world? Do you feel the undercurrent of creation's desire to honor the passing of the old paradigms and birth the new ones? Do you feel more able to step in the direction of imagination, collaboration, and creation when you have more of a solid foundation with yourself through the feeling of truth in your body?

Take a moment to dream. To vision. To wish. To hope. To believe in the highest expression of our new world to be birthed through each one of us. Each and every day.

Plant a seed in your heart.
Plant a seed in the soil of the earth.
Tend them both. Daily.
Cleanse and weed distractions.
Water and nourish the roots.
Cherish the growth.
Smell the flowers.
Plant more seeds.
They will feed this world more than you could ever imagine.

EMPOWERMENT

Our spirit is always in communication with us through the sensations of our body. When we honor how we authentically feel, we honor the spirit that animates us.

Your body is sacred and is what allows you to feel your connection to the divine spark inside of you—and in everything. Your body is also what makes your human life possible. We are first born when our infinite spirit animates our temporary, ever-changing physical body. And then, we *continue to be reborn in each moment* when our infinite spirit animates our temporary, ever-changing physical body.

Let's experience a moment like that right now...As you breathe in and out, feel your awareness of spirit enter your body with each inhale...Now, stay with that sensation of spirit embodied as you slowly exhale...

Many people have a soulful sense that they wanted to be here on earth during this evolution of consciousness in humanity. Would you be willing to explore the idea that an aspect of yourself is so courageous it would choose to be resilient to the challenges of this world and trust? Trust that in each cycle, phase and stage of life, it would be possible to choose to align with their soul's original intent to heal, embody love, and bring the consciousness of compassion to this world and to this time? How do you believe it is possible to stay soulfully empowered on this journey?

Wouldn't it be great if we had something to help us on our journey? How about a compass to help navigate the way?

Your body *is* this compass. The physical sensation of truth is your true north. Once you know where north is, you can locate all the other directions.

Of course we will all go into certain situations where we desire compliments, praise, or feedback to know that we are on the right course or need to course correct. However, when it comes to moving our body and embodying our soul on our spiritual path, things become more complex if they are rooted in the need for external validation. Be very wary of anyone or anything that points you away from the truth you feel in your body.

Just as the wisdom of the earth is always available wherever you are, an oracle full of teachings is available to you through your body. From your first breath to your last, your body is what merges with your soul to allow you to learn, grow, explore, and embody your essence in this world at this time. Many relationships in your life will begin and dissolve. There will be different romantic relationships, friends, jobs, homes, and places where you live. However, one relationship will be constant in this incarnation—the relationship between your soul and your body.

Explore honoring this feeling of empowerment by truly trusting the physical sensations in your body as you move into your day. You need not sign up for a special course to practice this. Start by simply feeling into your body as you live your daily life. Notice what crosses your path. The next time something challenges you to go against what you know to be true in your body, choose to honor yourself instead. Do an experiment to feel for yourself what it is like to consciously stand in your own internal validation, and one moment at a time, living with a sense of embodied empowerment.

GIVING AND RECEIVING

All nourishing relationships thrive in a reciprocal flow of giving and receiving. The more you learn to listen to your body and honor its messages, the more you receive access to the inner wisdom and creativity inside of yourself that inspires you to give to this world.

To expand your capacity for receiving the wisdom of the body, start by generously giving to it what it is asking for in each present moment. Many people's modern lifestyles are unsustainably orientated around negating their body's signals, deeming them inconvenient. An easy example would be when the body is exhausted and instead of giving it needed rest, one pushes through, likely with the help of large amounts of caffeine!

Doing what you need to do to get through the day is completely understable—and best when balanced with time for you to deeply listen to and honor the call of the body as it arises.

How can you give to your body today? Is it going to bed early? Having a 'staycation' at home? Eating a healthier diet? Daily exercise? Massage? Baths before bed? Nature walks? What would most deeply nourish your body today? Can you start to ask yourself this question each day and notice what it is like for you when you commit to give to your body as much as you receive from it?

EXPRESSION

Do you know that feeling when you catch up with a good friend and at the end of the conversation you really feel like you found the words to express how you truly felt? In the philosophy of Qoya as a movement modality, the goal is to reclaim that same ability to express oneself authentically through the language of your body. What does it feel like when you move in a way that expresses how you truly feel rather than repressing it?

On the journey of remembering how to authentically express yourself, a safe space is required. A place where you can imagine there is no way to do it wrong. The way you know you are doing it right, is that it *feels* right to you.

Think of a young child and the enchantment that surrounds them as they purely express their experience. Do you believe that it is possible for you to have people and places in your life where you can fully self-express as an adult?

It is imperative for the body to have time and space to explore its authentic expression and dance past the edges of its inhibition. When one embraces the original intent of the human experience to embody their soul, safe and sacred places where one is given continuous permission and encouragement are essential.

What is the risk in acquiescing to situations where there is not space for the truth to be expressed by you? Imagine the consequence of not prioritizing safe places for your body to explore its truth over time? Think of all the people who will benefit from your authenticity? If you are unable to create more space for yourself to feel how you really feel and express how you really feel, perhaps you are able to do this in honor of your family, friends, or those who will come after you.

The prayer is that as we claim these spaces for ourselves in our own lives the very best that we can, we also become models for others to have permission and the encouragement to express their truth in the way they move their bodies and live their lives.

INTUITION

If you want stronger biceps, then you practice doing bicep curls. If you want stronger intuition, then you practice listening to the truth in your body as you live your daily life. Instead of waiting for some monumental life decision to start strengthening your intuition, imagine every moment in every day is a great opportunity to pause before making a decision and notice the physical sensation of truth you feel in your body.

Listening to and following your intuition does not mean that you will be able to escape the normal challenges of life. It does mean that one of the main challenges will be that you didn't go against yourself. As we prioritize listening to the body's wisdom as a felt sensation of the soul, there is a newfound freedom to embrace one's journey as truly one's own.

Let's try it now: Think of a yes/no question that you have. Now bring your hands on your belly and notice as you ask the question if your intuitive physical sense in your gut expands or contracts? For many people, the expansion is a physical expression of yes and contraction is for no.

As you continue on the path of embodiment, notice what resonates with you and the physical sensations of truth that guide you on your path. Practice listening to them and encouraging others to do the same. So many of the instructions for positive growth at this time will be nonlinear body-based intuitions. Feeling more confident trusting your intuition is something that is best lived into and strengthened through experience.

EMBODIED ASCENSION

The spiritual path is often marked by the desire to ascend out of the embodied realm. In this philosophy, our human flesh is presented as a fiction, a maya, an illusion, and as a distraction from "more sacred" pursuits like striving to merge with a life beyond the one we see, hear, taste, touch, and smell in our daily experiences.

As we better honor the co-occurring realities of the physical world and the spirit world, we see them as not at odds with one another but as co-creative states of being that live in a conscious embrace. Instead of our spiritual pursuits taking us away from this world or our physical lives distracting us from spirit, perhaps honoring our spirit can be what inspires us to savor our embodiment, while savoring our embodiment will inspire us to be more reverent of the spirit that animates this body.

When the body is revered as home for the spirit, nature is also revered as the external manifestation of the world of spirit. The goal is not to only ascend our awareness up and out of our body, but also down and in to it.

When the spiritual seeds you plant are not only in the etheric realm but also in the home of your bones, blood, and breath, your soul experiences true homecoming. Without your body, your soul cannot do its service here on earth.

Are you in? Are you in for proclaiming, "To embody the transcendent is why we are here"? If so, I invite you to speak it aloud with your voice into the room where you are three times:

> To embody the transcendent is why we are here.
> To embody the transcendent is why we are here.
> To embody the transcendent is why we are here.

And then, I invite you to say that same sentence somehow through the way you move your body. There is no way to do this wrong—and the way you know you're doing it right is that it feels right to you. How do you speak the sentence you just said aloud with words through the movement of your body?

It has been an honor to share this dance of words together and if you would like to continue exploring these philosophies of sacred body wisdom together, I have devoted my life to inviting people to dance with these ideas through a movement system called *Qoya*. Qoya is based on the idea that through movement, we remember. We remember that our essence is inherently wise, wild, and free. *Wise, wild* and *free* also draw reference to the movement forms that we do in each class.

Wise calls on the wisdom traditions and contemplative practices of yoga, meditation, breathing, and intention setting that connect us with our inner wisdom. *Wild* calls on the authentic expression available to us in dance when we choose to express versus repressing ourselves. *Free* is about expanding our capacity to enjoy being in our body through more feminine and sensually based movements where we explore focusing less on how it looks and more on how it feels, with the knowing that there is no way you can do it wrong and the way you know you're doing it right is that it feels right to you.

In many ways, Qoya classes are a school to develop internal validation based on trusting one's own intuitive embodied wisdom. In Qoya classes, there are no compliments and no corrections because the point of class is not to look a certain way or learn a particular technique. The intention of a Qoya class is to remember your essence. To feel the sensation of the eternal aspect of your soul find home in your body.

May you be blessed as you continue your journey. And may we embody the transcendent a little bit more today because we have danced and because we have gathered together to remember.

Rochelle Schieck loves to move in her body and around the world. Over the last 20 years, she has traveled around the world as a student and teacher leading over 4,000 movement classes, training hundreds of Qoya teachers in 20 different countries, and taking women on over 70 retreats to sacred places in North and South America, Europe, Africa, Asia, Australia, and New Zealand.

Her passion to explore the emerging essence of the feminine in her own life and in movement, coupled with her experience as a personal trainer, certified massage therapist, shamanic energy healer, and her degree in Interdisciplinary Fine Arts, have all influenced her creation of Qoya, a movement system based on the idea that through movement, we remember. We remember our essence is wise, wild and free. *Wise, wild,* and *free* also reference the movement forms practiced in a Qoya class: wise for yoga, wild for dance, and free for feminine movement. There is no way to do Qoya wrong, and the way you know you're doing it right is when it feels good, when you feel the truth in your body and express it through movement. Rochelle's work has been featured in outlets like Oprah.com, Forbes, Self, New York Magazine, The Telegraph, and Psychology Today.

Qoya will celebrate its 10-year anniversary on March 1st, 2019. Learn more by reading Rochelle's book, *Qoya: A Compass for Navigating an Embodied Life that is Wise, Wild and Free* or trying Qoya yourself by doing the free "10 Days of Qoya Love" program where you receive a short Qoya movement ritual video to move with each day. Learn more at **www.qoya.love.**

Special Gift

Enjoy this free chapter of *Qoya: A Compass for Navigating an Embodied Life that is Wise, Wild and Free* and our e-course 10 Days of Qoya Love.
Both will be delivered right in your inbox after you sign up.

To access, visit:
www.qoya.love/free-chapter-and-course

Rise Like A Phoenix:
Braving the Storms of Transformation in Service to Love

BY LETTIE SULLIVAN

What do you do when you go through a health crisis so intense that you feel like a stranger in your own body? When what is happening is so extreme that you look in the mirror and don't recognize yourself? How do you navigate the storms that come from an unexpected health crisis?

In approximately nine months' time I went from being fit, strong, and active, to atrophied, infected, and weak, and then restored to a radiant, whole, and inspired human being. It was as though I had died, descended into the Underworld, and then was resurrected. Nine months—the time it takes to gestate a human being.

This is a story about the process of creation, destruction, and preservation—in service to my own personal growth and ascension. It's how I very deliberately invited in the storms of transformation and then rode the waves until finally reaching calm, yet exciting, new shores.

There is much talk of suffering across religious traditions the world over. Ancient wisdom teachings speak to the suffering of the world and that it is optional, illusory, and both necessary and unnecessary. What gets lost sometimes is that there are other definitions of suffering in the dictionary. Just like the word *surrender*, the word *suffering* gets a bad rap depending on which definition or understanding you use in your approach. It's time to turn suffering on its head so that whether it's your own personal experience or if you are witnessing your loved ones on their own journey, you can activate the energy required to overcome the circumstances creating the suffering.

The definition of suffering I will use in relationship to my personal experience is: To endure or undergo without sinking; to support; to sustain; to bear up under.

So, to suffer is to undergo circumstances without sinking and to bear up under the challenge of that situation. It speaks to buoyancy, resilience, and the ability to bounce back.

EARLY BODY IMPRESSIONS

My earliest memories of becoming aware of my body were from comments being said about me by adults that I was a "pretty little girl with big ol' legs." Church ladies especially would point out my "big ol' legs"—and not in a derogatory way. In my community, it was a common practice to describe people by their most unusual characteristic, whether that was big ears, buck teeth, big forehead, or dark skin. For some it amounted to constant teasing and bullying. To my young ears it felt like admiration rather than being made fun of. So that was the shorthand descriptor for most people when it came to me. After puberty when my interest in boys skyrocketed, my muscular body and "big ol' legs" were my calling card even more than the usual "big tits" and "big ass" comments made about other girls.

On my eighteenth birthday I joined the neighborhood fitness center. I can still remember the smell of rubber mats, metal, sweat, and cleaning solution. The air conditioning was cranked on full blast, and 1980s electronic dance club music was thumping through my body.

It was here that my commitment to fitness and strength in my body began. Being recognized for being muscular and strong affirmed me; I prided myself on demonstrating that strength. I would tell my friends or even new acquaintances to climb on my back where I would walk around and even do a few squats. Being strong was a central part of my identity.

All my life people called me pretty, but it was also tempered by "it's what's on the inside that really counts." So I fed my mind by reading voraciously. I embraced my religion and practiced being a "good Christian girl" by being obedient, mostly silent and self-contained, kind and meek. Being affirmed for being strong, I found, was even better than being called pretty and smart and good. To me, my physical strength was my greatest asset. Little did I know that there is much more to strength than muscles.

Reflection Questions

What are some of the earliest impressions you received about your body? How have other people's' opinions shaped your relationship with your body? Are you still relating to your body based on those opinions?

GOING TO THE NEXT LEVEL

Discovering the connection between the body and the mind took my training and conditioning routines to a whole new level. I soon learned the key role nutrition plays in maintaining strength and helping the body recover. By loosely using the scientific method, I tinkered with the process of finding the best food, supplements, fluids, and recovery methods to stay strong and healthy.

Then in 2003, the CEO of the company I worked for challenged the staff to train and run a marathon for a $1,000 bonus—and I was the only person who took the challenge out of more than 30 employees. For me, marathon training was the ultimate in mind/body training. As the training miles increase into the double digits, the mind must be stretched to push the body just a little bit further than it has ever been. And then you repeat that over and over again until you cross the finish line.

It was then that I learned very definitively how the body will do whatever my mind tells it to do—if I continually respond to what my body needs in the moment. This requires a constant dialogue internally with the symptoms being expressed by my body. While I was running I became intimately acquainted with what dehydration feels like and how to boost lagging energy. I learned the difference between a superficial cramp and pain that indicates an injury. I learned the contours of the expression of pain in my body.

I had a relationship with pain that became nuanced.
Agony and ecstasy ran on parallel tracks within my mind and
often crisscrossed while I was running.

The brain chemicals released during intense exertion, such as dopamine and epinephrine, had me hooked and coming back for more. I was addicted to exercise, and it consumed a good bit of my waking hours. Dr. Judith Wright described this phenomena as a "soft addiction," which is a repetitive behavior pattern that includes something most people find harmless, such as caffeine, shopping, TV, social media, or video games. During that period of my life I ran all year round, regardless of weather, and trained many others to run the Chicago Marathon and other shorter distances just to keep myself on track.

Reflection Questions

What are your "soft addictions"? Are there things you do that others find perfectly acceptable but that you take to an extreme? Do you attempt to hide from people in your life just how far you take things?

BEGINNING TO GO DEEPER

I have three children. The oldest are two years apart and my youngest came along six years later. All three were delivered via C-section. The pain of recovery from those procedures got progressively worse and longer each time. After my last child, I knew my running days were over. By then, however, I discovered the connection between the mind, the body, and my Spirit.

During my continuous marathon training, which took up a five-year span of my life between my late 20s and early 30s, I was introduced to yoga and breathwork as a way to increase lung capacity and flexibility in support of the increased demands I was putting on my body. It was purely practical and physical, at first. Then, when meditation was added to my yoga and breathwork routine, a doorway was opened within me and the dialogue with my body shifted.

I began to feel a kind of strength that was beyond exertion.

That new strength gave me the fuel to set my life on fire and pursue my dreams with gusto. I started my own business, traveled the world, climbed mountains, raised my children, loved my husband, served at my spiritual center, worked to complete my degree, and tended to my heart to heal old wounds. I was unstoppable.

Until my life hit the proverbial brick wall.

After a week-long hospital stay and a battery of tests, I was diagnosed with Crohn's disease in October 2013. No longer could I explain away the symptoms I was living with and bypassing with daily Tylenol. I finally had a label for what was occurring inside my body and even though I didn't like being labeled with a chronic autoimmune disorder, I set my sights on eliminating the underlying causes.

The first thing I had to face was that my life was over-scheduled and overwhelming. Never was that clearer for me than when I had to take a full hour to call and cancel everything in my appointment book because I had been admitted to the hospital. Call after call I made, realizing that my life was a runaway train that had derailed and I had a big mess to clean up both inside me and outside of me.

I had watched my mother be strong and "keep it together" through some of the most trying and desperate circumstances. She taught me what determination, resilience, and prayers could do. I watched her work herself into exhaustion. If my mother ever fell apart, she kept it from us. In that spirit of turning pain into power, I picked myself up, dusted myself off, and did whatever it took to bring that condition to heal. I succeeded in bringing the Crohn's into a deep remission using food as medicine and being supported by the best complementary and alternative medicine practitioners I could find. It was *not* easy, but I was able to maintain remission for four years.

Reflection Questions

Has your body given you signs to slow down that you've ignored?

CALLING IN THE GODDESS

Kali-Eh-Swa-HA! Rhythmic drums are playing from my iPhone speaker, my body feels *hot*. I'm vibrating, sweating, and dancing—my face smeared with my moon blood and streaked with tears. It's 2017 and I am all alone in my home. I dance and invoke the Goddess Kali to rise and cut the energetic chords binding me to the lineage of abuse, poverty, and conflict that had plagued my family tree up to that point. To call in a deep cleansing and

healing that would go forward seven generations and back seven generations, setting a powerful intention in a very deliberate way at a specifically
appointed time. I did it for my daughters, for my mother, my sisters, my
aunts, and my cousins. For all the women in our family lineage that had been
abused, mistreated, unseen, and unloved.

Because I had been spared the sexual, physical, and verbal abuse
during childhood, I chose to use my heart, my body, and my consciousness
to heal my lineage.

I invited in the Goddess Kali Ma to unravel the energetic ties that kept
me bound. I invited in the Goddess Pele to stoke my inner fire and passion
to propel me forward towards the fulfillment of my dreams. I prayed for discernment, guidance, and peace. I had an intellectual understanding of the
forces being engaged. While I had spiritual mentors that had been guiding
me for many years, this ritual was coming directly from my intuition, a part
of me that was streaming from the Unknown. I would soon find out just how
powerful this evocation would become.

GAME CHANGER

After my fortieth birthday, I set my intentions for the upcoming year. At
the top of the list was to get into the best shape of my life. I wanted to attain
optimal health and set about addressing some niggly health concerns that I
had been avoiding, like the molar in my mouth that had chipped and needed
a crown, or the low energy caused by my iron deficiency anemia. I've never
been a fan of hospitals and besides being admitted to have my three children, I had only been in the hospital once before.

When that declaration to get in optimal shape was made, I was at a
cruising altitude with my health. I felt I could lose a few pounds and tone up
but had become a lot less vigilant with the quality of my eating. My goal was
to halt the aging process in its tracks and increase my energy levels so that I
could be more creative and engaged with life and not so tired all the time. I
knew I had been putting crap food in my system, and I decided it was time
to halt the downward slide.

Unfortunately, after having the crown put on my tooth, I developed an
abscess and was given very strong antibiotics to treat it. I was in severe pain
and was using up to ten Tylenol a day, both over the counter and eventually,

prescription. Certain foods began to really cause digestive discomfort—sometimes almost immediately. It progressed from bread, pasta, and dairy products to just about everything. Since I was already taking painkillers for my dental pain, it also numbed the digestive discomfort.

Then the weight loss started. The first 8 to 10 pounds were welcome. I noticed my clothes fitting looser and my rolls began to smooth out. The second 10 pounds I lost had begun to limit my wardrobe choices to a few pair of leggings and yoga pants. People in my life were giving me worried glances, but I reassured them that I had everything under control and was getting treatment.

Little did I know that the treatments I was getting were prolonging the inevitable. I was going to have to face that Crohn's disease again—head on.

My intention to attain optimal health could not leave that condition unaddressed. I was scared. I knew it would be unpleasant and require a trip to the hospital. My primary care physician was helping me with diagnostic testing and referrals to specialists. My holistic doctor was giving me supplements to treat the inflammation, plus energy healing, homeopathy, and whatever else was in her bag of tricks that pertained to my symptoms. My Reiki practitioners went to work on my subtle energy fields and used crystals, sound, light, and aromatherapy.

I was throwing the proverbial kitchen sink at my body, to no avail. Not only did I continue to get thinner, my skin had taken on an odd, greenish tint. I had to put out a distress call to the women in my community for smaller clothes because within a span of 6 to 8 weeks I had dropped about four sizes. I asked if anyone had size twos and fours hanging around that they could loan me until I recovered. Now, everyone was really worried. I continued to tell myself that I had everything under control.

The last straw was being in my bedroom talking to my husband while getting dressed. I stood up from our bed preparing to leave for work and the next thing I remember was looking up and my husband was standing over me with unshed tears in his eyes. I had passed out. My very first time ever blacking out completely. The bed broke my fall.

Finally, I checked myself into the hospital.

DESCENT INTO THE UNDERWORLD

The surgery was scheduled for the Wednesday before Thanksgiving because obviously no one else wanted to have bowel surgery before the biggest eating holiday of the year. It was supposed to be a relatively straightforward laparoscopic procedure to remove a narrow section of my colon that included removing my appendix. It was soon discovered that something had gone terribly wrong.

On Thanksgiving Day, when many families were gathering around the traditional feast, food I had eaten that morning began to leak through a hole that had been accidentally burned into a healthy section of my colon. After the CT scan revealed the mistake, I was rushed back into surgery where my abdomen was cut open and my intestines were pulled out and thoroughly inspected to find the hole, repair it, and then rinse out all the gunk that had leaked out.

This set off a chain of events that left me hospitalized for weeks, withering away and isolated from my loved ones. I descended into a dark night of the soul. I suffered. I gave myself permission to be weak, to treat myself like a newborn baby and to allow others to do the same.

When in a deep healing process, I discovered it's not the time to project strength and that it is okay to "suffer." When I was laying in that hospital bed at 105 lbs, a full 50 lbs lighter than I was just months earlier, face and body akin to photos of concentration camp survivors, I fell apart. I succumbed to the voices of dread, fear, pain, anger, blame, and despair. The thoughts racing through my head caused my body to curl in on itself, and rivers of tears flowed from my eyes. Something inside me fractured, and what remained was a sense of numb compliance. It was then in my deepest moment of despair that I felt the presence of my deceased mother climb in the bed with me. It was as real to me as the pain lighting up my central nervous system. Immediately after the moment passed I grabbed my journal and this poem flowed from me:

This morning, I cried in my momma's arms.
I died in my momma's arms.

I let Her take to the Otherside
All of the tears that she couldn't shed

That I shed, for Her.

*I let Her take all of the fear that she couldn't show, that I showed
for Her.*
I let Her take all the burdens I carried for Her.

I cried in my momma's arms.
I died in my momma's arms.
I felt Her soft belly and floppy breasts at my back.
I felt Her breath and smelled Her cologne.

I heard the wetness of Her tears.
*I listened to Her song of Love grow distant as she took all I held for
Her to the Otherside.*

It was then that I knew that my work to heal my ancestral lineage
was complete and I began to ascend. Imagine trying to hold a beach ball
underwater. It just won't stay down because the water is surrounding it and
pushing it upward from every direction. Everyone in my life was praying
for me, rallying around my family and showing up for me in my time of
greatest need. I felt excruciatingly vulnerable, and yet allowing others to
care for me was a transformation in and of itself. Receiving this support
accelerated my healing.

My physical body has been strong and healthy for much of my life, and
I had to trust that it would remember and return to wholeness. Ultimately,
I employed all the healing methods and practitioners that I had used while
my health declined. This time their efforts supported me in restoring my
physical body, my tattered mind, and my tender emotions.

Slowly, like the Phoenix, I ascended from the ashes of my greatest health
challenge vibrant, radiant, and deeply compassionate. And now, my relationships with strength, resilience, surrender, and suffering have been forever changed.

Lettie Sullivan has been schooled by life, love, and a few universities. Also, through online courses, seminars, retreats, workshops, conferences and lots and lots of books. She loves her husband and children, extended family, and close friends and neighbors. Lettie is whole unto herself. A sovereign queen stepping in her power to support the establishment of a new social consciousness. A writer,

speaker, leader, mystic, and Practitioner. She is the Creatrix of The Goddess Ministry whose mission is to anchor spiritual practices centered in the Divine Feminine archetypes, metaphysical principles and lunar time cycles. You can find her on the full moon facilitating Goddess Gatherings. Learn more at **www.thegoddessministry.com.**

Special Gift

Healing Prayers

Prayer works! If your heart is heavy and you need to hear words of affirmation, healing, and encouragement, then take advantage of this special gift from Lettie. Whether you desire healing for yourself or another, or letting go of something or someone, there is a prayer here for you.

To access, visit:
www.thegoddessministry.com/healing-prayers

Real Then and Real Now

BY JEANNE ADWANI

Memories can be lovely to travel. They are what stories are made up of and passed along and down the familial trail of who's who and who did what and when. They can hold you tenderly, ecstatically, and woefully. They can wall you into their 'what was' and hold you trapped in a cage of yesterdays that keeps 'what is' from letting you live the fullness of yourself.

There is the story often told that when you reach a certain age, all you have are those memories. What was is never to be again, and what you are now in this aged and declining body, is without the juicy joys of youth. Society, in its collective limited thinking, gives all that to the young and leaves many of us over fifty-five humans, held to what we aren't as opposed to the juicy Wisdom Keepers that we are now. That is what we become. That is where our juice is now.

There needs to be a paradigm shift about who and what we are *now*. We have moved beyond the *silky smooth, hot and juicy, smart and sassy, 'the world is your oyster'* kind of thinking. This thinking limits those of us that are still All That in crappy skin, varicose veins, turkey neck, wrinkles of beauty, cuddly rolls of fat, penises that don't quite get it up, and pussies that take time to excite and get moist. You will get older and these body issues *will* happen and you will have to lament what was, and find your way to what Is. Youth will betray you.

Why not let age invigorate you?

This 70-year-old body temple holds so many memories. Some memories are resonant from some ancient time not perceivable in this time, some seemingly so present in the moment that I can smell the fertile exploration of them. I can close my eyes and teleport myself back into multi-sensorial times, breathing into those moments, reaching out and feeling the silk tendrils of the past wrap around me in remembrance. They settle into different places within me.

WHAT WAS REAL THEN...

I was fully invested in the 70's drug, sex, and rock n' roll scene.

The best of places and the hardest of places thrive in my body's sensorial remembrances. Some wander the once luxuriant ground of my womb of tender lovers—that sweetness of togetherness held to our heart's race to meet each other in a meld of higher love and ecstatic union.

And then there are us erotic thieves made for one-night-stands—those pick-ups that rob us of our own hunger. Stealing, taking, feeding from each other the vital life force of a wanton night or two—or three—in the crave to feel what our bodies might do in the stranger of us. Exploring the uninhibited spaces of deep penetration, of giving it All up to an outsider for the pleasures of letting them inside with no need for accountability. *Pleasure for the sake of pleasure.* Tempting the 'hands of fate' in the soak of sweaty sheets with the moans and screams held to strictly physical experience.

Sacred body land
Temple doors split wide open
Pleasures taken raw

Sitting here in this memoir of me that will lead you to What's Real for me now, I feel into those years; forty years ago and then some...listening and feeling into what every surface of me from skin to heart to womb has to tell.

My skin remembers the silky smooth of me. It remembers the ways many have touched me, caressed me in want and hunger, and left me begging for more, or have had me gather my clothes and leave as quickly as the hunger dissipates into "What the fuck am I doing here?"

Glistening shivers
Silky skin in wants caress
Beg me to love you

My ear has been fed and I have fed many an ear with whispering words of love and desire, the hard breathy nibble, and dirty talk of want.

Blow whispers in my ear
Breathe your want hard all over me
make me believe you

Sensations live on the palms of my hand and on the tips of my fingers. Remembering the exploration of hardening a lover's penis, moistening a swollen vagina and moving my fingers gently, forcefully, ecstatically on and in. Making nipples hard while caressing and licking breasts. Nimbly tying loose knots around wrists, in the restriction of touch, teasing, the surfaces of flesh while speaking of what might, what will, happen soon, very soon when the tease and restriction can barely breathe. And in the afterglow of climax there is the shared comfort in running hands over the shivering sweaty body slow to come to rest after multiple orgasms. And the aftermath of love making, holding, caressing, petting the beloved with tenderness and sweet kisses.

Feathered finger touch
Bound to wait a word release
Tease lust's surrender

My womb has held and been explored by hands, penises, mouths and tongues, by vibrators and objects safe and threatening. Pushing and probing at the vital orgasmic zones deep within and lighting up the fire of that little clitoral button loaded and exploding in ecstasy. The womb view has had the sacred and the profane all a swirl of pleasure and regrets. My womb remembers too much.

Sacred woman cup
Holy grail of becoming
Pull me from drowning

Ah...and then there is the kiss; the hungry mouth, the probing tongue, the exploring, sweet taste of a lover. Is it not in the kiss, the lingering mouth to mouth softness, the hardness, the fit of lips to lips and hot breath that begins the body's rise to desire?

If I were to have to choose what would be my singular hungry want, that can tease me into desire, it would be in the kiss. It is a wordless divine connection that can say everything. There is no foreplay more thrilling to me than the slow, tender, ravenous kiss. It can be a deep language of intimacy when the heart finds another heart open, and willing.

Find my lips tender
Tease the ripe fruit of my mouth
Taste at my portal

WHAT IS REAL NOW...

My Body Temple lives mostly in the reminisce of those yesterdays, as far as my physical/sexual self. Not because I really want to let the past wanderlust take me, and hold me ransom of what was. The *Be Here Now* part of me wants nothing to do with what was, other than for it to act as information and remind me of the wisdom I have collected and earned over these decades.

I am quick to be pulled out of a good *Now* moment when my body rebels against me, and I wish that being 70 years old still had me juicy and desirable. Age has found its way to shift my body's responses; how my body finds the desire state, how my body can handle sexual activity as it no longer gives of its moisture. The skin of my vagina is taunt and hard; Atrophied; unable to receive any form of penetration without the pain of ripping and bleeding. My clitoris is still ready and willing to receive and give; that little tip of my iceberg still waits and wants.

Might I love the folds and fat, the broken veins and crapping skin, the arthritic knees, the sagging breasts, the slow pull of gravity that sped up when "70" called the warranty of this body to another reality. I'd be a liar to tell you that I love how this body is now that she doesn't have that vitality and flexibility anymore. My mind says I'm 35 and my body speaks differently. It screams differently. It wants to scream ecstatically. I look in the mirror and I still see that sassy, creative girl, all full of herself giggling her way across the world, tasting and exploring the wonders of the Primal Goddess.

Ageism has become a gloom over some of us Baby Boomers. We are to make way for the young and up and coming. And yes, that's true...But *no*, not at the expense of diminishing ourselves because we've reached 'a certain age' and our intelligence, usefulness, and sexiness has changed. The massive gathering of wisdom that age naturally offers, if you're paying attention, can be shuffled away and deemed unnecessary, useless to the vitality of the young, useless to corporate America that has let our wisdom be pushed aside for the crackle and pop of youth. Retire us and send us 'out to pasture' and out of the way. Certainly, this is not an across the board experience, some of us are honored and appreciated well past that chronological warranty.

How do we, as Wisdom Keepers, still get to be 'juicy' and appreciated in our vibrancy and wealth of Knowing? Our wisdom is not limited to the wealth of information that we have gathered—it lives in our whole body. My mind is very very sexy.

And let's not kid ourselves; after menopause, and the change in life that men pass through, society says we are *not* sexy anymore. Our 'parts' certainly don't do what they used to do; all shriveled and nasty (shame on those naysayers). And who wants to talk about that? Who wants to challenge that story line? Do you want to speak out loud about your vagina, when it's not working as you imagine it should cause it to be a hot and tender, moist and hungry bit of a sex toy? You are 'shoulding' on yourself, and holding us all to that paradigm of limited thinking about sex and aging. Are you going to buy into that myth or are you going to make a declaration to change it?

So I say, where is the community of the many of us done with our menses, or have had their womb removed as a result of illness that took certain hormones out of the luscious mix of body want? Some of us hide out because we no longer have the hormones that gave us the juicy, stirred up body desire, keeping us moist and tender the way youthfulness did. Some of us lost the 'fuck like maniacs' factor, or the 'gentle tenderness of making love for hours' factor. Aging bodies change, the loss of hormones shift the desire nature, and now who and what are we? Are we somebody's wife, partner, grandmother, mother? A singular living alone? How do we move into this new body, this new self that has to grieve what was and embrace what is? Who do we talk to? How do we speak out loud to our partners, our friends about this new self and what we need *now*? How do we stop the strangling story that says now we're old, we're crones, we're hags, dried up and certainly not desirable or sexy anymore?

I am a changemaker. And it's time to get uncomfortable with shifting perspectives about sex and aging. I am NOT that granny who wishes to be dismissed and unnoticed in her advancing years. I am a new kind of sexy and desirable and that needs to get talked about and acknowledged.

This body temple is an expression of the Divine Feminine. I AM rising to make her known and clearly stated in the world. I get to shift perspectives of how women are imagined into being. I get to break useless old paradigms that limit us, and refresh and renew how I wish to thrive and love in this world. I get to be all of what I imagine myself to be as I bring a shift in how power over is no power at all. I get to proclaim that my body is still desirable and sensual. I don't have to hide in the background on behalf of youth placed ahead of me. I get to speak out loud about sex and the desire state of being. I get to be 'full of self' in this world I inhabit, and be a reflection to others of we who find ourselves diminished by ageism.

My 'new' intimacy is wrap around kissing and holding, hugging and tender touch, teasing and talking dirty, licking and sucking, talking about what stimulates my partner and they to me. Curiosity and the 'what if' is a great playground for infinite possibilities. And maybe thrills are experienced in the wonder of nature, and the conversation of infinity and the great beyond of what I can not see or understand; that glorious Liminal spaciousness. Why can't that be the new sexy? It sure can be sexy to me to have conversations that take my mind out beyond what I imagine possible. Whatever *feels* sexy is what needs attention and conversation. There are many ways to get to an orgasm, whether it's at the tip of my clitoris, deep inside my womb, or in the spaciousness of my expanding heart and mind.

So sisters, we 'GET' to do this as out-loud and as quietly as we want. We get to make a new kind of magic—an Alchemical brew of intimacy and Love. The point is, we are the ones we have been waiting for. Me. You, We, are The ONES. Now is the time to tend to the garden of our souls and body. Love what is now and grieve what has lost itself to youth. Nurture how this body is in its new marvel. How magical it is that we have lived this long? We have gathered so much knowledge, wisdom, and the opportunity to have loved deeply, loved many, loved on ourselves. We 'get to' reflect all that out in the world to shift this new paradigm into one of sensual, juicy, sovereign Queens at all ages.

What is done for One is done for All.

Wholly Is

Wholly is the temple of my bone and sinew
The tempest of false body image that
Have suffered the old stories of what isn't
Traveling the harsh road of those false myths

Failing in the tender of what Is that needs regard
No matter the way age thinks to ravage
Trying to lessen the Infinite of wholeness wisdom
Ever present with lullabies and sonnets

And yet, this Temple of heart and breath
Finds a way to thank gravity and breakdown
For the gifts of wisdom left in the deterioration
Giving prayers of wholeness, healing and well being

What revenge could be sweeter than to
Wrap the arms of love around this body temple
Take gentle fingertips and caress those
Mounds of tired flesh and gravity's sag.

Feeling into the hidden moist
Where the Sun can not go and
The Moon's glow lays remembrances
Of juicy and lustful want.

Wholly is the Temple of this Body
Aged to perfection, simmered in
The cauldron of Wisdom's Keep
Boiling away what isn't
Bubbling and brewing All that is

Jeanne Adwani—I am an artist/creat-rix, a Muse, a poet, a Creativity Coach, a Light and energy shifter, a Sister on the path of the 13 Moon Mystery School. I am a hair 'healer,' owner of a salon called "Be Hair Now", and co-creator of the beautiful experience of Evenstar's Chalice in downtown Ypsi-lanti, MI. I am taking and making a deep  dive into the experience of becoming an Anointing Priestess; creating a line of essential blends called Sovereign Elements.

I hold the space on this Earth life for paradox; that standing between the worlds of duality where Love and fear share the same space, at the same time, and need the same balance.

My roots are deep in Earth-based Spirituality, honoring the Divine Feminine as we rise again to nurture, celebrate, and empower All life with Love and wisdom.

I listen to and play with the magic of the elements that are around and within us all: Earth, Fire, Air, Water, and Spirit tell our stories, and connect us to the sacredness of all life.

I access the energy and 'stories' of tarot, numerology, astrology, and the deep listening to Spirit and silence to find a path to an under-standing of personal wisdom and self-empowerment.

It is my 'Heart's desire' to practice the Path of Love, peace and kind-ness, in the "Be Here Now," to laugh as much as possible, and 'To turn to love no matter what'. Namaste'

Visit my poetry blog at **www.geezergirl.org.**

Rooting Grace on Earth

BY EDEN AMADORA

The darkness is not sexy. It's hard to talk about. We don't want to feel our feelings—especially our discomfort. We're programmed to use addictions to numb, to medicate.

We don't want to "look there," yet it's profoundly needed. We live in a world where there's an increase of suicides and kids killing other kids. More and more people are on painkillers.

You can see why our western culture is only three days deep—meaning that many of us don't have the tools to be in the darkness, in the unknown, for more than three days, like Shamans do, in order to receive oracle and become initiated.

We don't want to feel the collective despair, let alone our own.

Yet, that's what's required—to *feel* it. To integrate it. To be willing to go *four* days deep within ourselves and traverse the wilderness, be with what is there, and let Spirit bring back grace to touch us.

We must be able to go *all the way into our bodies and feel everything* in order to truly be embodied and receive the gift of grace into our being.

The upper chakras are easy. I used to live about a foot over my head, and I think a lot of us in this New Age culture are floating. But that's just spiritual bypassing.

We're obsessed with ascension because we don't want to feel the pain of being human. And while there's a lot of talk about bringing heaven to earth, I don't think many of us realize the initiation it requires. It's a deeply personal journey into loving our shadow as much as our light and *literally* requires making a descent—a deep dive into the darkest part of ourselves.

It can feel deathly quiet at the bottom of the well. It will scare you. Can you trust the darkness? Can you find the spark in the center of your heart that will guide you through?

I didn't trust myself for years. I didn't know how to listen to my heart. I didn't even know how to be fully in my body, much less honor it as sacred.

My body was a product I used and sold to gain the admiration and love of others—to get what I needed and wanted in the world. I completely identified *as* my body.

I blossomed into puberty and became a lingerie model at age fifteen, standing in rooms full of strangers staring at me as a sexual object and cash cow because of the shape of my body and the way I looked. Boys and men responded to me in a way that made me feel powerful for the first time in my life. I loved being desired and looked at. I loved the way they reacted to me. The attention felt like love. So, I used my body like a commodity.

My entire source of self-worth hinged upon being desired and wanted—whether it was for sex, love, or money. It *was* power—and I felt alive. But, I wasn't truly alive. I wasn't present. I was mostly afraid, just surviving. I felt separate from my true self, from Source. There was only ego.

I sold myself short and I sold my soul many times in the heart of the darkness of the glamor world. I compromised my truth and essential self, with no sense of inner guidance or boundaries. I was polarized into a shadowy part of my inner feminine, the seductress archetype in order to feel any connection or semblance of love.

We break our hearts open again, and again, and again with the choices we make.

I held a long pattern of being with men I knew were not healthy for me: the emotionally unavailable "bad boys." But for me, being desired meant being safe. If I could reach out and "get" love from men—play the game right, be beautiful and alluring—I'd be taken care of.

Despite being a model, I held a wave of deep self-judgment, shame, and insecurity about my body. Now, I see all the ways I didn't feel whole and aligned, how I didn't cherish or value myself. I looked into the mirror of others to find a reflection of my worth.

This pattern needed to shatter.

ଔ ଔ

A breakdown might just be the breakthrough we need—the chance to finally go all the way in and through and take responsibility for our part of our story. That's the medicine of the Hindu deity *Kali*.

She asks, *"When are you going to stop giving away your power and making others responsible for you? How much longer are you going to reach outside looking for validation in the mirror of another of your worth? How many times are you going to play the victim?"*

And she takes me on a journey.

ଔ ଔ

SHATTERED HEART

Even though it's been years since my fashion modeling days, and I've been "modeling" a different pattern as an ecstatic embodiment guide and priestess who stands for self-love, and supports other women on their spiritual journey, I find myself on my knees again.

My body aches. I'm lying on the floor in my pajamas at 5:00 pm on a Friday evening. My heart hurts. I'm experiencing a really traumatic break-up with my partner and beloved.

The irony, after years of being seen as most men's idealized, desired body type, I called in someone to shatter this false sense of power, humbling me, as he rejects me based on not being his physical "type."

How could he not accept me when I earned a living
off this body?

In the mirror of his reflection, I am not enough, and an old, primal shame resurfaces: Am I not worthy of love? It feels like my body has been hit by a truck; I'm in physical pain—the pain of withdrawal from this addictive cycle with my dysfunctional lovership.

I see how paralyzing, annihilating, and abusive my inner voices still are; I've been spending so much time and energy leaking power, projecting on and blaming the person I feel victimized by—the one who "broke" my heart.

I thought I'd be in a different place in my life from where I am now. Everything feels like it's collapsing upon itself: All my facades, strategies, and plans. I'm humbled. I thought I had already hit my bottom and was on a steady ascent toward the sun.

I want to be out of this hell realm, but I'm in the underworld, in the darkness again. It smells wet, fecund. I feel fear in my root. My toes want to recoil from the slime.

There's a whisper of a song coming back to me from the past; it's ancient and haunting—indigenous—with a steady pulsing drum beat:

> *Hold my breaking heart, don't stop now.*
> *Hold my aching heart.*
> *Go deeper.*
> *Hold my waking heart.*
> *It will free you...*
> *It will crack you open.*

The back of my heart feels shattered, blown open, broken. It's as if it was once a beautiful, stained glass window that held stories of a radiant, golden sun, shining its rays down upon an angel, holding a child—holding this divine child light of innocence—next to an image of beloveds: a noble queen and king lifting up an overflowing chalice of love and plenty.

That stained glass heart was once luminous and intact, but now feels blown open, like there are pieces missing in the picture...like a window in an old, abandoned church, once resonant with song and rituals of devotion... now silent and dusty with roosting pigeons.

I'm in the bottom of the well with a shattered, stained glass window on the back of my heart, looking into an abandoned, barren church, on my knees, breathing shallowly.

Uncomfortable constriction wells up inside of me. I carry a core primal fear and disgust—even shame—about my past, about my sexuality, about the way I've used and abused my own body. The dense vibration of self-loathing and shame scrapes the bottom of my heart. From somewhere really far away, I hear that hypnotic drum beat building. I hear that haunting song.

I know it's inside of me, yet it feels like it's sourced from something "out there," pulling me and guiding me onward.

I've been here before.

Every time I hit this darkness, this bottom, this grief, I forget. I forget how painful it feels. I forget that this is the depth that's within me as a soul. It's mine...to mine.

So, I crawl.

And that song: *Hold my breaking heart, hold my aching heart, hold my waking heart* keeps repeating silently on a loop. I'm crying out for someone else to save me from this state, to comfort me, to hold my bones to the ground. If only there was some external relief for this deep inner ache...

Here, in the bottom of this dark well, I find a tunnel, an underworld chamber that I begin to traverse. I'm pulled slowly, laboriously forward, by the drum beat of my broken heart. I breathe deeper and start trusting the unknown journey...little, by little.

This is my life, this is my creation, this is my journey. Can I love myself here in the disillusionment, in the despair? Can I just hold myself here?

ᘓ   ᘓ

I remember an echo of a story about how the wound contains the blessing, how the shadow transmutes into the gift, how our suffering is the key to grace, how you cannot have light without darkness. I hear:

Humble Nobility and Noble Humility.

The truth is, I like to feel like the sun, like a lioness on top of the world. Nobility feels empowering, sexy, and easy for me to embody. My Leo rising loves to feel bright and shiny, special.

It's the humility I never really understood; I never really knew what that meant to embody.

ᘓ   ᘓ

CRAWLING IN THE DARKNESS

Tapping down deeper into the underworld, crawling along, feeling the wet earth, smelling the dampness, brushed by cool roots, I feel humbled into a little creature, like a belly crawler.

I'm asking, *"Can I still love myself like this, too? Can I love this being I've become in this moment on my journey?"* My body says:

Just put your belly on the earth, mama.
Crawl...crawl until you learn how to walk again.

Just let go.
Let go of your ambitions.
Let go of your cares about what it looks like.
Let go of what they think.
Let go of what you think you need.
Give it up.
Let go.

Oh, I know you. Hello, Queen of Death.

Her cool touch lands on my back heart and it's soothing. It's soothing to those jagged shards of glass, soothing to dissolve them and to let go of all the pretty pictures.

...To let go of the angel, the divine child Christ pictures, the lovers—even the blazing sun. Let it go. And just be.

She strokes my back heart with her cool, silky, light touch and says, *"All of it...let it go. You can even cough it up. Let the sorrow in your lungs come up. Let go of the dream."*

SHADOW WALKING

Another presence arrives—an old, crusty hag. It's dark, but I feel her cold, bony hand grip my arm. It's Duhmmavahati, an aspect of Kali, Goddess of Disillusionment, of Grief, of Despair.

She releases a kind of death rattle and says, *"Get up. It's OK. You can still move forward in the pitch blackness, without knowing."*

She guides me, slowly, step by step, and we start to sing.

"Hold my breaking heart;
hold my aching heart;
hold my waking heart.
It will...crack you open."

She says:

Even though you think you've been here before, it's a little deeper every time. You've never really been HERE before...for you have carved out more capacity to feel.

Just as your lion heart reaches up to expand and embrace this whole world in loving radiance—as much as you stretch your prayers up to the stars—you're being asked to go in deeper now.

Get down to the bare bones, the minerals within them.

It's time to go down deep within, to let go of any more attachment to who you think you are and of how you think it should be.

ଓ ଓ

This is about healing, integrating, and wholing all polarities, especially my Divine/Primal split—this part of me that would rather be in Spirit and not on this plane, not in a body, because it's too fucking painful.

ଓ ଓ

Remember, little one, you signed up. You signed up for this. You said that you want to bring heaven to earth. Start within your own being. Bring your love to the darkest, tightest, ugliest, loneliest, most desolate, aching places within yourself. That's where it begins.

You already know that nobody else out there can 'save you.' So, every time your mind wants to conjure up a victim story and judge, put your belly back down on the earth.

Give it up.

You can give it up quick or slow: It's up to you. There is no one "out there" to blame.

And, by the way, your shattered, stained-glass heart is not real. You painted that picture. That is an illusion.

You act out the victim and the shatterer again, and again, and again. It's only your projections and expectations you're shattering—to make way for **GRACE**.

 C3   C3

When I'm disembodied, I'm not present. Instead, I react, feel like the trau-matized victim, and don't want to be radically accountable to my part.

With her quiet rasp, she asks when I'm going to be ready to give up seeking—seeking anything outside myself.

C3   C3

The more you reach out of your center, seeking—that experience, that beloved, that apparent blessing, that accolade, that success, that amazing invitation—whatever it is you're fantasizing about outside, over there, if, when...believing then, you'll be happier, more fulfilled, whole—you are chasing an illusion and you are leaking power.

You are forgetting that everything begins within.

Everything.

So, be where you are, beloved.

Be here.
In this.
Now.
In the discomfort.
In the unknown.
Each shaky breath—a portal...
Within your own body.

Love when it is not pretty.
Love when you are stripped down to the bones.
Love when you are alone.

Remember, remember your deep magic.
It's here in the dark, at the root.

Your suffering is the key.
You know better than to resist or deny it anymore.

You must go in and through.

There is so much beauty and power to be mined—fuel for your ascent, for your evolution.

So, walk in beauty child. Even here. Now.
Especially here...in the darkness.

And know this: Your heart is not made of glass; it is as vast as the cosmos.
When you really get that, you become a world maker.

This is your mythic story, your heroine's journey.

Go deeper...
Deep, deep inside your belly.
Deep, deep inside your yoni.
Deep, deep inside your root.

Deep, deep inside each sole chakra of each foot.
And below that...

Bring us the real gold...
Rooting Grace on Earth.

Eden Amadora is a speaker, coach, mentor, and spiritual guide. She is a featured author in *The New Feminine Evolutionary: Embody Presence—Be the Change.* She is a master facilitator, archetypal channel, mystic, and muse.

After 20 years of yogic and shamanic training, Eden found her heart at home in the 13 Moon Mystery School. She is now an Ordained Priestess, ecstatic embodiment guide and initiator, witnessing the life-changing transformations that occur in her ceremonial spaces working with the archetypes of the Divine Feminine and initiating men through embodying the archetypes of the Sacred Masculine.

As a ceremonial facilitator, sound healer, and prayer-formance artist, Eden also enjoys leading sacred song and ritual circles using sound and voice as an alchemical tool for transformation.

She is highly regarded as a pure and seasoned "presence of transforming love" and raises a uniquely effective call to awaken our authentic selves. Learn more at **www.edenamadora.com.**

Special Gift

FREE MASTERCLASS
Awakening the Sun Heart: 3 Keys for Women to Call Forth the
Sacred Masculine and Heal Our Relationships with Men

Beloved, come, heal the wounds of separation and create harmony
with the masculine during this activating, free, online class.

Many of us have suffered from the very deep and painful wound of
feeling separated and disconnected from the masculine; because of
this wound, we often experience relationship struggles with men.

And now, women and men are yearning for connection that's
rooted in grace and transcends the old stories.

Are you called to create more authentic, harmonious, and
satisfying relationships with men?

Are you ready to call forth the Sacred Masculine Essence?

If you feel your heart screaming "YES!", I invite you to join me for
this very powerful, free online masterclass where we will dig deep
into this topic.

You can join here, beloved:
www.sunheartfoundation.com/masterclass

dreamWeaving One Heartbeat breathing

BY LYNETTE CANNON

dear Reader, Come!
can I tell you a Story? ...a Story of Wounding
and a Story of Healing ...a Story of Hope
and a Story of Soul full Whisperings
whispering ...*Remember!*

and so it was just the other day resting quietly and forever so gently imagining *before* ...and *beyond* ...Doorways ...within Doorways ... aeons unfurling ...and she wondered

What is it all about?

Who am I? Why am I here?

C3 ...CB ...CB

and in her deepest reverie ...she remembers the fey One telling her

~~there is but One Heartbeat
dear Childe, be that Heartbeat!~~

ॐ ...ॐ ...ॐ

and SlipShifting Realms ...The Poet stands now at The Water's edge

and Here ...and there ...playing quietly ...all by herself ...she watches a young girl building a magnificent Sandcastle

~~and moving closer
The Poet wonders why she is playing all alone~~

ॐ ...ॐ ...ॐ

and looking up ...the little One meets her eyes ...and she says

~~I'm always alone
everyone always leaves~~

then ...with a Gaze of exquisite Innocence

~~so what I do is something to make them go
because they go anyway ...so I get in first ...and then they go~~

ॐ ...ॐ ...ॐ

and The Poet listens deeper

and deeply deep Within ...she *Knows* ...the care not I ...so very brave ...so very sad little girl ...playing quietly ...building her Sandcastle ...on the beach ...all alone ...is her

and moving closer now...wrapping her close ...snuggled up against her body ...The Poet asks the little One for a sign to let her know when she is moving away

ॐ ...ॐ ...ॐ

CB ...CB ...CB

and tenderly ...and forever so gently ...within Love's deepest embrace
...the little One touches her left cheek

and transcending Space ...and transcending Time ...within The
Mystery of The Dream ...The Poet meets The Touch

~~and with her left hand
she touches the little One's hand touching her left cheek~~

CB ...CB ...CB

and Soul full Whisperings
quietly whisper

Essence ...at essence ...in essence ...is All
no need for the labels ...or separation into parts
beyond Mind is Flow ...expansive ...and raw

within The Rawness breathes sophisticated Integrity
Order within Chaos ...and Chaos births Order
always, within Essence ...The Centre holds True

The Centre holds True when all hell breaks loose
illusions shattered ...identities dead
only from The Centre can Truth be upheld

Truth upheld ...already foretold
it's all in The re-Membering
ancient Future ...re-Called

CB ...CB ...CB

and there are some Moments in Life that are truly Life altering in their consequence ...some we know shall be so in the moment we face Choice ...others unVeil their mysteries as time goes by

and so it was ...many Moons ago ...week 5 of a 6 week public speaking workshop ...*The Temple Journey* from the recently released album 'Medicine Woman' wafting its magick into the Seminar room

ભ ...ભ ...ભ

and she walked In ...apologizing for her absence the week before ...and briefing her on The Plan for the evening

~~present a 2 minute Talk on childhood play~~

dear Reader, hearing those words ...her life ...as she knew it ...was never to be the same

head down ...eyes slammed shut

blackness descending ...a kick in the guts

her arms wrapping around her belly

holding her ...comforting her ...protecting her

no sight ...roaring sound ...she was no thing ...and no where

seconds felt like aeons ...and inside she was trying to find something

anything ...she could talk about

ભ ...ભ ...ભ

one Inquiry ...one Intent ...one Instruction ...and the unraveling began

~~ the wound of a Woman ...Thy Healing has begun~~

and dear Reader, in the days to come so many things in her life began to make sense ...as bit ...by bit ...she pieced together a very different story of Summer holidays at The Seaside

and in her body ...feeling Memory

the step Up ...through the door ...into the caravan

playing for The Camera ...out of the caravan ...through the door

the step Down ...and she hadn't been there ...it never happened

and remembering ...it's too much for others to hear

so she keeps it all inside ...and she tries to forget she remembers

~~and she leaves her Truth to fit into where she does not belong~~

CB ...CB ...CB

and The Coldness floods her ...cold to the core ...her bones feel cold ...her Heart feels cold ...her head hurts ...she feels frightened ...she feels lost

and when The Terror overwhelms her ...she retreats ...and falls apart

~~help me ...she screams
rescue me ...take away the pain~~

and it's cold in this place where she feels so alone ...scattered energies ...moving ...moving ...doing anything ...*except* being Still

~~emotion floods through her ...she goes numb
she doesn't want to feel ...frozen ...and stuck in time
there's no Light ...it's heavy ...and it hurts~~

CB ...CB ...CB

CB ...CB ...CB

and she who is so very tired is who she is ...Here ...and there

and she who is so very tired is so very angry
and she who is so very angry is so very sad
and she who is so very sad grows cold

and she who grows so very cold ...sinks deeper and deeper ...deeper and deeper ...sinking ...and shrinking ...holding it all together ...and falling apart ...so much pain ...it hurts ...she shuts down

and tenderly ...and forever so gently ...within Love's deepest embrace... the little One touches The Poet's left cheek

~~and transcending Space ...and transcending Time
within The Mystery of The Dream
The Poet meets The Touch~~

CB ...CB ...CB

and weaving into The Deepening ...The Poet remembers it all began with a Hawk and a Dove ...that fateful Date with Destiny ...so many Moons ago

as she sat in her corner office ...on the 11th floor of a tall glass building ...so terribly unhappy ...so lost ...devoid of all Hope and Purpose ...her Faith in The Goodness of Humanity sorely depleted ...she watched a Hawk circling amongst the buildings in the city centre

and she looked past ...towards the hills ...in the far distance ...*beyond*

and walking in the following day ...there ...on the ledge ...the bloodied mess of a grey Dove ...scattered ...ripped apart

~~and in her body she *Knew* she was looking in The Mirror~~

ଓ ...ଓ ...ଓ

and in that Moment ...that eternal Moment of Infinite Possibility ...*before* ...and *beyond* ...aeons in The Making ... dear Reader, there was no choice ...other than The Choice ...to step Free

and in the coming days Life conspired to support her as she initiated her own Redundancy

and meeting with the consultant recruited to offer transitioning service ...she heard him say ...almost as if to himself ...very Feminine

~~as if her being Feminine
somehow explained the entirety of misfit~~

ଓ ...ଓ ...ଓ

and she made no sign of having heard his words

and she never forgot them

and such depth of pain was entangled within internalised projections of The Guilt ...and The Shame

ଓ ...ଓ ...ଓ

and the fey One Calls ... breathe Still, dear Childe

~~journey with Us ...don't fear Us
The Light is above you ...around you ...and through you
We hold you Close ...you are not alone~~

ଓ ...ଓ ...ଓ

CB ...CB ...CB

and in that eternal Moment of Infinite Possibility ...dreaming The Dream
of One Heartbeat breathing ...The Poet re-Turns to a Time before

~~to heal the wound at its energetic Core~~

CB ...CB ...CB

and so it was that Night ...many Moons ago ...re-Patterning Future
...re-Visioning Past ...The Poet speaks Clear

I'm out of touch with myself
it's time to take back control

steering my direction ...calmly Clear
True to Soul ...and all I hold dear

environments defined by Others
it's time to take down what they have put there

replace the space ...strip it bare
an empty canvas ...prepared with Care

Possibility ...emerging from The Chaos
harness The Energy ...forge new Creations

draw forth The Power ...summon The Light
Sacred Space ...Safe haven ...for re-Visioned Sight

CB ...CB ...CB

ᚼ …ᚼ …ᚼ

wounds of Separation …wounds of Love

~~I Name you …and I release you~~

dis-Membering *The Silencing* …dis-Mantling The Shame
with each Worde spoken what you have been unravels

dis-Membering *The Silencing* …dis-Mantling The Shame
with each Worde spoken what you have been dissolves

dis-Membering *The Silencing* …dis-Mantling The Shame
with each Worde spoken what you have been evolves

wounds of Separation …wounds of Love

~~I Name you …and I step Free~~

ᚼ …ᚼ …ᚼ

and the fey One Calls …dear Childe, *Remember!*

it is not necessarily the way she stands …or the clothes she wears
it is not necessarily the weapons she holds

The Power comes from Within …and is never compromised

she can be pushed …she can be shoved
but The Power is still there …The Strength …and The Glory

The Power of One does not need to control Another
for The Power is a Strength of its Own

the power Source remains Constant
and doesn't get damaged by The Pushing ...and The Shoving

∞ ...∞ ...∞

and within The Mystery of The Dream ...transcending Space ...and Transcending Time ...so it was that Night ...many Moons ago ...head bowed ...wheelchair bound ...quietly waiting ...the wounded warrior waits

he who Stole ...and denied Sovereign Presence ...manipulating within her woundedness ...waiting quietly ...the wounded warrior waits

∞ ...∞ ...∞

and within The Mystery of The Dream ...transcending Space ...and Transcending Time ...in her hands ...she holds an ancient black Vial

and The Poet steps closer ...and quietly she Asks

~~would you like me to Lift you Up?~~

and as she speaks ...The Vial falls to his lap ...and in her hand now ...she holds a Needle

and head bowed ...a quiet smile ...the wounded warrior stands ...and quietly ...He steps forth

and within The Archway of Light ...He meets her eyes ...and within The Light of Love ...she Receives His Gaze ...and He turns

~~ re-Turning ...One ...within The Light~~

∞ ...∞ ...∞

CB ...CB ...CB

and within The Mystery of The Dream ...transcending Space
...and Transcending Time ...gowned in ancient Robes ...a Man stands
Presenced ...and He bows ...and He says

~~that was a very Noble thing you just did~~

and The Poet meets His Gaze

~~and an ancient Memory begins to awaken~~

CB ...CB ...CB

and within The Mystery of The Dream ...transcending Space ...and transcending Time ...she hears Vibrations of Sound

and turning ...One ...by One ...a Gathering of Others form a Line...and
with heads bowed ...quietly they walk slowly by

and the fey One Calls ...dear Childe, Come!

CB ...CB ...CB

and in that eternal Moment of Infinite Possibility ...with Conscious
Choice ...The Poet steps In

~~and she watches she who she has been

take the little One's hand

and Together ...they walk to The Centre of an ancient Wheel~~

CB ...CB ...CB

℀ ...℀ ...℀

and Soul full Whisperings
quietly whisper
do you *Remember?*

in the blink of an eye so long ago we stepped Away

we yearned for more ...it was necessary for Our growth
we split into Two ...and began Our Journeys ...in Parallel

a Yearning ...a Hunger to re-Turn Home
often Nameless ...un-Named ...and un-*Known*

many Lifetimes ...many wounds
Eternity ...transcending Space ...and transcending Time

℀ ...℀ ...℀

each Lifetime planned before we Arrive

Experiences ...lessons and learnings with Others
woven specific to Our Soul's Plan

embedded aetherically we have multitudes of Choice
déjà vu ...is awakened Memory Rising

℀ ...℀ ...℀

~~and Veiled within The Shadows of The Mirror
shines The Light of Our Truth~~

℀ ...℀ ...℀

CB …CB …CB

and so it was …just the other day …resting quietly…and forever so gently breathing The Dream of One Heartbeat breathing

SlipShifting Realms …The Poet opens her eyes

CB …CB …CB

~~and transcending Space …and transcending Time
within The Mystery of The Dream
The Wheel of re-Turn turns~~

CB …CB …CB

and
so it is
dear Reader
We are done!

Lynette Cannon A mystic Storyteller ...and transformation Guide ...eyes open to Vistas behind The Veil ...the lived experience of Soul re-Membering has challenged, trained, and guided Lynette through many rounds of illness, injury, and trauma ...and gifted her with many Moments of Grace full re-Calibration to The Sacred Centre.

As if a Dreamer awake she walks between The Worldes ...dreamWeaving Worde magick as her Sacred Tool of Trade.

Her Soul's Code, 'elegant Simplicity ...embodied ...and breathed ...eloquently and evocatively speaks its Truth through the medium of mystical Storytelling.

Continuing her transformational collaboration with Flower of Life Press, Lynette is fine tuning her inaugural book, *The Priestess ...her story ...and an ancient Memory of Power* due for release March Equinox 2019.

...and dreaming into the next Story ...gently calling, Come!

Learn more at **www.mysticalstorytelling.com**

Thunderbolt of Lightning and the Nature of Alchemy

BY DIANNE CHALIFOUR

Fierce Mother, like a strike of lightning, would come to penetrate the crevices of my being. "No, you have not gone deep enough daughter. Forgiveness."

"Forgiveness of what?" I ask.

"Can you feel *what this little girl felt? Or is she so locked up and hidden away for safekeeping that you would have no idea how to access her? The life-learned skill of numbing out parts of self once served but is now a burden and no longer comfortable. A vessel already full cannot receive substance. Release. Unlearn!"*

My opportunity to release and unlearn the numbness arose through a rage releasing practice in sisterhood. By experiencing old pain, Fierce Mother has afforded me the gift of releasing, deeper than ever before, emotion stored deep in my body, to allow this little girl inside of me to finally let go of what she had been holding for so long, safely hidden in the vaulted chambers within the vessel of my being. This Fierce Mother, an archetypal energy of the Divine Feminine, is one I have come to deeply honor as a catalyst for transformation. She is but one face of many to help me navigate the ever-changing terrain of my life.

Holding onto pain is our ego's unconscious strategy for survival when afflicted by the suffering of others. In this way, the pain somehow seems manageable, tolerable, perhaps even non-existent. It serves as a defense mechanism to continue to operate and survive despite outer circumstance.

It's quite a clever survival mechanism! However, eventually in some capacity, this holding serves the container no longer.

"Clench your fists sisters!" the facilitator yells. "Feel rage held in your body, your own rage, collective rage of the feminine!" I allow the rage to well up, and then, "RAHHHHHHH!!!!" I let it all go with the flinging and shaking of my arms, moving and screaming, releasing until I feel energy coursing through my body, fire ignited, raging storm welling up. "I AM DONE WITH THIS SHIT!"

Inertia! I'm not even entirely sure what "THIS SHIT" is at this point... It's energy. Emotion. I feel it! Energy that has been stagnant, held within. I become aware of it. And now I seem to have made some agreement, on some level of my being, that it is time to let it go. It is time to empty the vessel to receive something new.

I now know we are here together to do the work, to release the wounds of the past that have held us prisoner in our own bodies. My own shadow work arises to my awareness as unresolved anger and rage. In reality, the tidal wave has only just begun. My words this moon would become the words of Her—Fierce Mother. Truth, left unsaid. Not sweet, not kind, compassionate truth but raw, raging truth from the depths of my soul.

Those closest often become the targets. In actuality, the holographic nature of our life invites the perfect scenarios for Divinely orchestrated entanglements. The nature of alchemy requires pressure to unearth the gold. We don't always see it coming, and we're not always able to contain the pressure, or even play nice. Being with what is real in each moment allows "truth" in that moment—the gold to come into form. My own unspoken truth comes from many places: My childhood, relationships of all kinds throughout my life...All serving as teachers for my soul's growth. I am humbly grateful to each one, even when first appearances may seem otherwise and they may be met with my own resistance.

She fires back in the face of what feels like accusations, "RAHHHH-HHH!!!!" I feel attacked with words. Except the fire inside has been ignited long before these actual words have been spoken to me. The apparent attack is yet another catalyst for release, for the truth held inside to be spoken. And later, reflected upon. *What is actually real in this situation, and in my words? I ponder. Where is this rage coming from?*

Retreating to a desert island or a mountain top retreat would seem the safest for me about now. But that's not the way it works in the mystery. We walk within the world, amongst the initiators of our lives, those we love, strangers too...any of which are suspect, any of which are triggers that hold the keys, mirroring back to us the raw truth of what must be uncovered to experience true freedom. For freedom is not what we most often think it is. It is not merely some superficial feeling of having no restrictions placed on us.

Freedom lives within the heart, and freedom requires us to find it there.

Freedom cannot be bought or sold. The moment we try to own freedom from the external, we become imprisoned by it. Freedom is far more expansive in nature and calls for alignment with our own integrity.

The vow of the modern-day Priestess, one who is in service to the Divine, is to walk as love—even amongst chaos—and to serve from this place. But walking as love means that all the places that are not love will become illuminated, with light cast upon them—like the illumination of the moon in full bloom—to bring us back to the only thing that is real: Lasting. Love. My heart, my soul, through this vow, naturally wants to bring me back to love, again and again. To honor what has come up from my depths to be released and transformed into gold. Into love.

After our rage-releasing ceremony, I became aware of the little girl inside me seeking freedom. Over the next few days, my left arm would progressively become almost completely immobilized. X-rays and exams would rule out any physical cause. I am well aware of my shadow work underway—the unresolved anger and rage. Years earlier, I'd lost my gallbladder to stored anger. For two years I resisted recommended surgery. I felt more anger with the suggestion that this organ given to me by my creator must be removed—that somehow I was failing myself! Eventually diving in meant honoring this part of my body that had held onto stored anger for as long as it could. Did I really need to keep perpetuating this old scenario?

"Emotional," says my Chiropractor, after the exam and somatic testing. By this time I have gone through almost an entire week with the use of just one arm—with sleepless nights and throbbing pain. It becomes a hyper focus. *Pain.* I've always considered myself to have this high pain threshold, and now I clearly see how this no longer serves me. A high pain threshold is not a badge of honor, contrary to the distorted masculine view.

And now the Fierce Mother has come to tell me, "Stop! It is time to feel the pain, the anger, the rage. You are no longer that scared, confused little girl. Now entering your wise woman years, you may not pass this point. Time to feel the pain body. Once it served you to hold this pain to keep you safe, and quiet. Hush little girl. But now it's time to release it. You cannot take it with you. You cannot know forgiveness without feeling all that feels unforgivable. Betrayal, abandonment, manipulation, distorted love. All common place to the little girl inside."

These were the first programs creating neural pathways of conditioned story. My path in life has brought me to such a place that I am able to more clearly see the old, distorted stories that have played out through my way of being in the world. Now with eyes to see, I am equipped to begin to reprogram my old story into a new one based in trust and love. I know that my life has been my teacher, and wisdom will arise out of the ashes of what was—like the Phoenix, renewed.

Completely consumed by the discomfort in my arm, I have no option but to go into the pain. My left arm, the feminine side of the body, lends the first body wisdom clue as to where to look to the root of pain. I feel myself slipping into despair, into a sense of hopelessness and victim energy—an old program running. And yet I trust. I am no stranger to accessing courage from a deeper knowing within me. I just know unmistakably I am held always. I have come so far now, there is no way I am not fully supported still! I know I must dive with my consciousness into my pain body, to allow it to have a voice. To embrace my shadow and *feel* the intense pain. I am so ready! I desire freedom!

This process has served as a significant catalyst for me to heal childhood wounds—perhaps even lifetimes of wounding—to step into wholeness and the essence of who I truly am, rather than continuing to wear the masks I have learned to hide behind and that have kept me locked in fear, projecting my wounds onto those closest to me. Once I began to taste freedom from the masks and the fear, I wanted more!

Once I learned to own my shadow, I realized this was the way to reclaim my power.

On the eve before the full moon in my own sacred temple space, and in the lunar energy where release is amplified, I sob, and scream in pain.

And then the little girl inside speaks, "The voices of a thousand women, ringing across time and dimension," my flowing pen informs me. "Failure and worthless." I feel weary, stressed, exhausted, and sad—so incredibly and painfully sad. I know I must land here in this moment allowing whatever comes forth onto my journal, to clear a very old story. The conditioned story. It's time for a rewrite.

My childhood years were filled with confusion and dysfunction. I didn't have sisters, but was gifted with five older brothers. I felt deeply, but had no voice, faithfully experiencing laryngitis twice a year around the solstices. I was always asked to speak up so people could hear me. I was afraid and often felt alone and different. I was ashamed of my family dynamics, as if no other family had their own share of dysfunction! When I was about six, my parents went through a bitter, ugly divorce. My mother had no tools to navigate this territory. Neither did my father, for that matter.

Fierce Mother speaks again. "It's time to tell the story, the story you have held for centuries of the abandonment and betrayal. The wounds of separation and judgment, of the screams and the cries heard across echoes of time from the women who feared their power, their strength, the courage to go beyond the walls that divide. You stand at this gateway, beloved, and we support you. We implore you to tell the story for your ancestors. The bloodline is deep and rich. We will guide and protect you. Fierce courage. Through pain and sorrow. You need not fear. This is your healing journey and this is the healing journey of a thousand women or more across lifetimes. You have known this in your bones and now they ache for the story to be told. Now is the time, Beloved."

I recall my mother often whispering about the women in our family and the gifts of knowing. She whispered this to me as if we were to fear that someone might find out. Like everyone else in her life, I mostly dismissed her ramblings as part and parcel of her alleged "mental state." I felt confused, yet there was something beneath the surface that felt more like rage. I was afraid. My voice fell silent. I shut her out, like everyone else had. I had to. But she was my Mother, and I loved her.

"There is no agony like bearing an untold
story inside of you."

~MAYA ANGELOU

"We are the voice of a thousand women, ringing across time and dimension. When you came into this world you held the sweet essence of Divinity. Fear began to set in quickly when you felt a different frequency. It was not love and you took it as rejection, abandonment. You only wanted love. It was within reach yet so far away. The love was missing long before your arrival, passed on down the lineage through fear, betrayal, and abandonment. As you grew you faced challenge after challenge, all rooted in separation, to match the division of the people from Source. But Beloved, the codes within your cells have never been taken from you and never can be. They are there, holding your gifts, the keys to assist in the awakening of the masses. The story is so rooted within the fabric of humanity it is no easy undertaking, and so you join with so many like you, all carrying their own unique threads. There is no more time to waste, Sister. Go within to activate your own codes of remembrance."

Born in Salem, Massachusetts, I have always been familiar with and intrigued by the "witchcraft hysteria" of 1692, while, at the same time, being repelled by anything to do with "witchcraft." On so many levels, it never made sense to me. Casting spells and manipulating circumstance to one's own will? But then there were those who offered plants as medicine and guidance through connection with an inner knowing. Were some pure and some not? This sense of dividing or separating one from the other reminded me of my Mother's deep devotion to her Catholic upbringing while also feeling shame and inner conflict related to her beliefs. "This is God?" I often pondered, "Something that would make her feel so much shame? And she must go through a man to connect with her own spirituality?"

"As you ran through the fields, breathless, exhausted, in fear for your life, and the life of your beloveds, you suffered at the hands of the Patriarch, beaten and abused. Left to die, tears streaming down your face. Yet there was he who found you, who gently picked you up and carried you to safety. Who healed you with herbs and the gentle energy of sunlight. He, who prayed over you, who knew the connections, the magic, to Gaia. For he was not of them. He, who holds the key of the Sacred Masculine who has never forgotten the wisdom and

sacredness of the womb. Who would never forsake such magnificence. Through time, however, he has been tainted, worn down, becoming the oppressor, forgetting who he is. Humanity stands at a threshold where the women must awaken and remember their gifts of healing, of presence, of fierce love and commitment, and the untainted Mother energy, to stand in her fierce courage and remind him who he is, who she is. Our survival is at risk. It is time to stand in courage and risk it all for love's sake. Drop the ego's perfectionistic desires about doing things just so, all neatly packaged with a pretty little pink bow. There's no such thing, Daughter of the Flame! Perfection is a distorted viewpoint; in truth lies integrity of deep truth and bold presence. When you ride the waves of integrity, all will unfold as it needs. Do not fear the darkness; the darkness will lead you where the eyes cannot."

I am blown away by what is coming through. The images flood my mind. I sob, and my body shakes as the words pour out of me as if from the very air I breathe. The little girl inside has been holding a long line-of-lineage story. My body is the vessel for the alchemical process of transmutation. The story is clearing through its surfacing from the depths of my body.

"The roads here are less traveled, hence the state of humanity. Your pain, Daughter, is all the times you wanted to speak your truth, but held it in for fear of being blamed, judged, ridiculed, or silenced. When the women gathered together in Temple, it was commonly known among one another that voices must be kept low. There was a silent revere that the women held inside. The Sisterhood. It was no longer safe to reveal the gifts that once had served all mankind. Once darkness set forth across all the lands, the voices of the women were hushed. A transformation of the ugliest kind began to take shape—the abandonment of our own integrity and all that we had been given as a birthright. All that threatened those who had already given over their own valiant integrity in favor of power, dominance, the shadow of the masculine."

Yes, I do know this story. As a child, in the whispers of my own mother, the wisdom I saw in my maternal grandmother's eyes, and the stories my aunt shared after my mother passed. "We are actually sisters, you and I," my mother told me, many times. I never quite understood the stories shared in sisterhood, the very sisterhood. I had no idea why I was so compelled several years ago to be part of the mystery school teachings and the path of awakening through feminine consciousness. The patriarchal structure from which we have operated for so long has brought us into deep imbalance. Men and women alike have suffered.

"And so it began—the silent rage that has coursed through our blood-lines for thousands of years. Thousands of years! From our mothers, and our grandmothers, and their mothers and on and on before them. This silence and shame of who we are at our core has become so bur-ied beneath the soil of Mother Earth that we've largely forgotten our own knowing, and the rage has been building for a very long time. We've held it in our wombs locked away even from ourselves. We have abandoned ourselves. Only now, She is awakening, and the pain, shame, sorrow, grief is being uncovered. It is time we stand together in our shared pain, to speak it and acknowledge it."

I pray to The Great Mother, the She in God, the Goddess. "Mother," I sob, "Please, take this pain from my body, my arm. I don't want to hold onto it anymore. I give it all to you, my pain, my doubt, my fears." It's an exhaust-ing experience of surrender. Hours later, I lay law, annihilated, and struggle to pick myself up off the temple floor. My face stained with mascara, I drift listlessly into sleep.

In the early morning hours, I journey home...not only to the home where walls keep me safe in bed at night but the home that knows I am held always in God/Goddess' perfect love and protection. This is the home I am really journeying to, that would eventually become clear.

Throughout the next day, doubt lingers, and I cannot help but wonder if I have made it all up. As the thought challenges me, suddenly I hear *"Crash!"* A dish is accidentally dropped in the kitchen, smashing to the floor. Subtle tremors course through my body...trauma...cell memory and I hear, "No, you have not made it up."

Collective rage releasing! We can't make this shit up! Releasing for our-selves, for our Mothers, and their Mothers. On and on it goes!

Images come into my awareness of my eight-year-old self, unable to escape the rage and fury of my broken mother, hurling and smashing every single thing in the house. Every dish shattered, fragmented, like the little girl with nowhere safe to run. Like the little girl within my own Mother—fragmented—and her mother before her—fragmented. The collective rage of the feminine. It's all beginning to make sense. This is the path of the initiate in the mystery. The vow to clear and to reclaim all the parts of self in order to walk as love.

My parents weren't able to see their way through the thickness that engulfed a marriage of a couple decades. Somewhere beneath it all, love existed; it was just too difficult to access from the fragmentation that ran down the line, to sort out what was actually theirs. Instead, the rage passed on like a family heirloom, woven like an invisible quilt that lay upon us each night while we placed our weary bodies to bed. These threads, meant to keep us warm, connected us to the stories passed generation to generation, the matrix that has become our modern-day family model.

As the days unfold, my strength is growing, fog slowly lifting, pain almost entirely gone. The masculine becomes my teacher, I'm soon to realize. It's all about the challenge, and the breaking down to come together in a new way...the very nature of alchemy.

On my way back to owning my power, all must be released to stand fully in my authentic essence. It's not the power of the wounded masculine. But he shows up in many faces to show me what he looks like and feels like so that I know how to properly integrate my own masculine energy in a healthy way. *The healed feminine must find balance with the healed masculine.* Her light reveals his shadow. Another bolt of lightning crashes into my awareness. It becomes clear where I have been giving my power away in masculine relationships. I'm still playing out the story of the lesser, paying it small, and diminishing myself to uphold the collective story so intricately woven into the matrix we have been plugged into for centuries. This is my part in the suppressed feminine. I have allowed it.

The truth is, not only have I been hiding out but I have supported the masculine in staying comfortably masked. I have played the part of needing to be rescued, at times dumbing myself down as a way of allowing him leverage, withholding to avoid tension, remaining on the surface more often than coming with an open heart. Upholding different standards for the feminine versus the masculine. I see that in order for our world to come to a more balanced state we must each integrate a balanced state within ourselves. We are both masculine and feminine. The perfection comes in the dance of life, where we learn to hold on, and we learn to let go as needed.

All at once, I see it everywhere. As I clear up the stories, I am able to come back to love, to come back into my body with gratitude for the teachers who show up on the path. It's the alchemist's gold. And I have struck the jackpot once again. Digging deeper, courageously with a hunger for truth, the truth has not been withheld from me. My heart is filled with gratitude for the pain that serves me on a soul level. This is my path! I could not know wisdom without embodying my life experiences. I cannot know compassion without feeling the pain first and holding it all in love: compassion for myself, compassion for others. Through the eyes of compassion, there is nothing to fix. True compassion brings everything into love, sees through the eyes of love, and invites forgiveness.

I know this experience will bring me closer to a deeper forgiveness of my own mother wounds. Forgiveness of what? Perhaps the forgiveness I am truly embarking on is self-forgiveness. To free the little girl inside to the wonder and joy of childhood. Freedom from guilt for shutting down and shutting love out when all she was doing was protecting herself.

With clearer understanding, my boundaries are strengthened and my capacity for love expanded. The journey is nowhere near complete but the power of my newfound understanding and wisdom rests like a cloak upon my soul. Awakening deeper, the larger picture becomes clearer now. I see the magic at play where I am brought into the temple of higher learning within the vessel of my being, and my own sacred body wisdom operating across all dimensions of time and space through this expanded lens.

Next stop on my alchemical journey: intimacy.

With all that has been released and the walls I have been dropping, I see the distortion in what I have always thought intimacy was. I have known intimacy only through sexuality. Eyes wide opened, I see that intimacy is the open-hearted connection that breathes life into all relations. The places I dare to be seen and to see and trust to stay present, no longer hiding, afraid of being seen. Instead, showing up completely raw, naked, masks unveiled. Loving myself fully and intimately with the desire to share more of myself and emotionally allowing others in. I now see how common it is to fear intimacy. We walk around guarding our hearts, masking our emotions, afraid of being seen, of being hurt, of connection. I feel the challenge in this new place I have never known. I am here again, tapping into my body wisdom to guide the way through to the alchemist's treasures. And, having laid to rest the victim story, I trust. I have been here countless times. She has not failed me. Only served as teacher, like those who would come to mirror for me. And so I allow myself to feel intimacy in relationships. I'm trying it on, noticing where I still wobble, where others shield themselves. Holding compassion for self, and for others. This intimacy serves me to know myself more fully and to hold space for others. I feel a softening and a freedom in this new place. I feel alive, no longer imprisoned in sealed off chambers of my heart.

My body is my wisdom temple, and she shows me the way to myself, the full, embodied presence of all of who I am. And I love her. Finally. I understand what *self-love* means. I understand that I can forgive on a much deeper level than I could in the past. With my heart expanded, and understanding the power of vulnerability, I can now begin to rewrite the story.

Dianne Chalifour is a writer and transformational guide within the healing arts, assisting her clients in connecting deeper within themselves. She owns a wellness center on the New Hampshire coast, a product of her passionate calling to offer tools and services to assist in the awakening, connection, and shifting of our human evolutionary process of living a soul-inspired life. She  guides sister circles where women come together in a safe space for inner work and re-connection with their feminine body wisdom.

Dianne is a passionate, compassionate leader who helps individuals—therefore, the whole—in bridging the disconnect within structures that hold us in a model of separation, to a more expansive, cohesive model that is calling us forward into a new way of being together in harmony in the world. She serves as a type of midwife for her clients to reach deep into their own inner knowing and step forward empowered into the life awaiting them.

In balance with her passionate engagement in her work, Dianne enjoys spending time in nature, in quiet, peaceful reflection and with her husband, three children, and two cats.

Learn more at **www.earthharmonywellness.com.**

The Tiger's Treasure

BY WINDY COOK

The water ripples below,
The waves shimmer,
snake like, deceptively serene.
The rocks rise up behind me,
Jagged, like my breath.
I glance down at my bare feet
I know what I have to do.
I don't have time,
to second-guess myself.
Why am I here?
As I feel the plunge,
my lungs cave in,
feeling the pressure.
I struggle to find the surface.
I glance to my left to get my bearings.
How far down am I?
Our eyes meet. I'm in the golden iris of amber.
A sacred space,
Fire and memory.
The tiger is suspended in the water,
swimming next to me.
I feel a surge of adrenaline.
I am terrified.
Time is in slow motion, how do I run away from a swimming
tiger?
"Just swim," a voice says, "Just swim."
So I do.

TIGER MEDICINE (1 TEASPOON OR 2, AND HOW OFTEN?)

I wake to the sunlight streaming in my bedroom and am reminded that I was just dreaming. The moment of relief washes over me like the first morning's shower. *What was that all about?* I ask myself.

> "To understand the concept of medicine in the Native American way, one must redefine 'medicine.' The medicine referred to is anything that improves one's connection to the Great Mystery and to all life. This would include the healing of the body, mind, and of spirit."
>
> —*JAMIE SAMS, AUTHOR OF* MEDICINE CARDS

Animal totems have always fascinated me, but I'm not familiar with tiger medicine. *Is the tiger one of my animal totems? Why haven't I known about the tiger being with me before? Why now?*

One of my animal totems is the owl. I've been gifted owl feathers through the years, and I dream about the owl. Several owl feathers grace my altar at home, and I have embraced the owl's spiritual gifts of vision and insight. I'm all too familiar with the nighthawk being able to see what others cannot. I also know about self-deception and that, like humans, animals have a shadow. I have the psychic sight, but I sometimes don't want to see what I fear, so I don't look.

I've never encountered a tiger except for in captivity, and I haven't dreamt about one either—until now.

Is it safe to look?

I look. I look to mythology and come face to face with the Mother goddess Durga, also known as Shakti or Devi. *Durga,* which means "fort" or fortress in Sanskrit, is the Hindu goddess of protection. Sitting astride a tiger or a lion, Durga battles, with her multitude of arms, the forces of darkness and evil. Durga takes on nine different forms, each of which embodies special and unique powers.

I have two arms, and Durga has at least eight. That is a lot of arms. What would I put in eight arms? I would have labradorite and amythest to deflect negativity, a rose to sweeten the air and calm my fear, a sword of truth, a goblet of water to quench my thirst, sage to cleanse the space, herbs to heal my inner child wounds, a candle to see in the darkness, and my sacred, wild untamed heart. The one heart of compassion and love. That one is the most powerful tool against evil. The weakest arm would hold it. Riding the tiger holding it all takes this to a whole new level. No wonder Durga is a goddess. Imagine what you could do with eight arms!

"There is great healing occurring in you Windy," says my friend Alis, who is from Cambodia, where the tiger is a powerful symbol. "The time for *you* to step into your power has come."

Tears find my cheeks and it's hard to exhale. I've been holding so much in and now it's time to exhale. To let what's been hidden, out.

Out with a ROAR.

This "roar" should be a developmental, normal process, right? As I reached womanhood at the age of twenty-one, I should be empowered, mature, and embracing my "goddess" self. Just like when you're sixteen. You get your driver's license and you can drive a car. Why do I have to step into my power? Where did I lose my way?

During the #MeToo movement, I was compelled to share my story of how I gave my power away at the ripe age of twenty-one—how it was *taken from me*. He was twice my age, claimed to be a shaman, and had *much to teach me*, he would say.

And he did. He taught me. He taught me all about what it feels like to trust someone who takes advantage of you in every way possible.

Why did I trust him? Where was my precious intuition, my inner voice?

But my inner voice failed me...void and unavailable.

My self-blame is evident, strong, and relentless.

Looking back, my voice didn't fail me. It whispered those words of warning. "Don't trust him. He is not who he says he is. He will betray, take advantage of you, and use you as he wishes."

But I didn't listen.

I didn't listen to my *body*.

I wasn't tuned in to *where* I should listen. I didn't listen to my inner core of the third chakra solar plexus, the seat of intuition. I didn't listen to my gut, my very own precious, life-saving intuition.

For others, I've heard, intuition can reside in other places in the body such as the throat or third eye. Where is intuition for you? Where in your body can you feel it? I wish someone would have asked me that question when I was coming of age.

The details of this time in my life when I didn't listen to my intuition are dark, but I let the light in and have since shared my story openly with others.

The support that I received from countless people was amazing. I let go of my shame...that it was my fault. And I felt lighter.

What path did you take when you didn't listen to your intuition? Where did you go?

My path has eventually led me to the tiger. Or did the tiger find me? Was the tiger a sign that I had retrieved my intuition and my personal power? Was sharing my story and releasing my shame the initiation I needed?

THE TIGER'S TREASURE

As we sit around the table in Sandi's kitchen, we share a laugh again as old friends do, and talk about our busy lives being moms. "Let's either open up a bottle of wine or take the high road and pick a card," Sandi says with a broad smile, and I nod in agreement. Each of us picks a card from the Louise Hay deck of inspirational quotes.

I pick a card and turn it over to see the message. "I stand on my own two feet," I read. "I accept and use my own power."

The words float up off the table like smoke from incense and I get goosebumps. I tell Sandi and Julianne about my recent dream with the tiger. With big nods, the room becomes silent and Sandi gives me that look of recognition and deep soul to soul acknowledgment.

I feel like I'm in my own mystery. I want to know more and find out why the tiger visited me in my dream.

I will never be quite the same. It's like the tiger and I exchanged something and it left a mark on my soul.

My fingers dial the number to the DragonTree spa. "Is Patrice available this week to do a massage?" I ask. Somehow I know that talk therapy isn't going to answer my questions and get deep enough. Intuitively, somehow I know that having a massage and bodywork will unlock this mystery and I will have clarity about the tiger and my dreamspace.

My mind flashes on a map that I learned through an online mentorship program called Journey of Young Women. The program offers a certificate of completion, and the course teaches how to empower girls, mentor young women in their "coming of age" and facilitate Moms and Girls Circles. The course offers practical wisdom, provides recommendations for resources, and instructs mentors to lead circles and activities in a guided "map of well being." The map of well being encompasses a comprehensive guide to physical, emotional, social, and spiritual health.

Interestingly, the map of well being begins with the *body.*

The body. The physical body is the foundation for everything and the very place to begin when mentoring girls and teaching about personal power. In my studies, I learned that it is paramount that we teach girls to view their body as a sacred, *sovereign* being, also known as *body sovereignty.*

Katharine Krueger, creator of Journey of Young Women, defines body sovereignty as, "The respect and inner knowing of one's own body. Understanding how to honor, protect and care for one's own body by being able to ask the question, 'Who gets to touch my body and come into my personal space?'"

I didn't learn this in school, and my mother didn't teach me either. She didn't give me a "doll" as in *Vasalisa the Wise,* that I could *feed* and tell me who to trust and who not to trust. My retrieval of my intuition was altogether different. My retrieval was feral and animalistic. I didn't know that my "doll" was my own *wild* body.

Have you ever noticed how animals are in the *now,* and they are acutely aware of their senses? Smell, sound, touch, and sight, not intellect, guide them. Their very survival depends upon it.

As girls, we were taught to doubt our truth and to disregard our instincts and emotional intelligence. We were taught to be "nice" and do what we were told. Girls are made of sugar and spice and everything *nice,* right? Do you remember someone telling you to cross your legs, say please and thank you, don't laugh too loud, do what you are told? I do. I wanted to take my shoes off, play in the dirt, jump like a grasshopper, and put dandelion chains in my hair.

Clarissa Pinkola Estes, author of *Women Who Run With the Wolves* writes, "We may have been taught to set aside acute insight in order to get along. However, the reward for being nice in oppressive circumstances is to be mistreated more."

My reward was superficial and my conditioning effective. I functioned primarily in my head. I had a constant voice telling me how to act, what to say, and what to do to be a good girl. I had become completely cut off from my body and my senses and what my body was trying to tell me.

My body that had weathered over forty years of life wasn't "tuning in" to my senses anymore. What I was smelling, what I was seeing, what I could hear, and what I was touching and feeling, or in other words my "wild" instincts. I was a grown-up woman with a "nice" girl running the show.

I remember as a young girl, whenever I asked my mother a challenging question about life, she would look at my father to hear him answer first. I often wondered why my father didn't look to my mother to hear what she had to say first. I grew up believing that men were smarter and knew how to answer complex questions better than women. Don't get me wrong— my mother went to law school and became a successful attorney—but she looked to my father for answers, especially the answers to tough questions.

> "Every woman is a portal, a shaman with a connection to Mother Earth—especially on the days of our moon time."
>
> —*KATHARINE KRUEGER, JOURNEY OF YOUNG WOMEN*

Interestingly, the aftermath and emotional scars of the early dark chapter of my life had to be healed physically. I had to have a physical release for the wound to heal. My gestalt therapist gave me a tennis racquet and told me to hit the pillow. "Hit the pillow as hard as you can and for as long as you need to." And I did. I hit that pillow until my arm throbbed and my body ached.

A well known resource held my hand and was my friend: Dr. Peter Rutter's *Sex in the Forbidden Zone: When Men in Power—Therapists, Doctors, Clergy, Teachers, and Others—Betray Women's Trust*. This book validated my experience and how strong the magnetic pull is when someone that is in a position of authority takes advantage of you. For me, this was easy. I was taught well to be really *nice and not to question authority*. This book gave me permission to let go of the shame.

CB   CB   CB   CB

I'm on the massage table. The smell of candles and the sound of falling water permeates the dim surroundings. Patrice asks me where my body needs attention and if I have any injuries that he should be aware of. I tell him that I've had a recent dream about a tiger and I don't know what to make of it all.

He nods and I know he understands. I knew Patrice would know. Patrice has been a massage therapist for many years, but he also integrates shamanic work and he understands the different worlds of the animals and the Great Mystery.

As Patrice begins to massage my lower back, my exhale indicates that I am finally beginning to relax. Patrice slowly works up my spine and something remarkable takes place. The massage table becomes the bark of a tree. I feel the bark of the tree as I climb higher. The tree's branches become the forest and I feel the roots spreading deep in the soil. My body grazes the tall grass and the leaves brush my throat. I have become the tiger and the tiger has become the forest. I am one with it all.

I am the tiger.

"Intuition has claws that pry things open and pin things down, it has eyes that can see through the shield of persona, it has ears that hear beyond the range of mundane human hearing. With these formidable psychic tools a woman takes on a shrewd and even precognitive animal consciousness, one that deepens her femininity and sharpens her ability to move confidently in the outer world."

—*CLARISSA PINKOLA ESTÉS, PH.D., AUTHOR OF* WOMEN WHO RUN WITH THE WOLVES: MYTHS AND STORIES OF THE WILD WOMAN ARCHETYPE

How can I help my twelve-year-old daughter confidently navigate through a world of choices and challenges? How do I help her, and other young women find their way back home to their feral instincts, their senses, and the Wild Mother, the precious instincts that have kept us alive since the beginning of time?

Can I protect my daughter as goddess Durga does, from the evils of society and the "all knowing authority" that coerces her into believing it has something to teach her? Or asking the deeper question of how to protect her from her own inner darkness of self doubt that is lurking in the societal messages embedded in her daily life? Is it about waiting for an animal to visit her, or for her to connect to the animal inside of her?

What animal has visited you, or were you the seeker?

"Intuition is the treasure of a woman's psyche...like a crystal through which one can see with uncanny interior vision. It is like a wise old woman who is with you always, who tells you whether you need to go left or right. It is a form of The One Who Knows, old La QueSafe, the Wild Woman."

—*CLARISSA PINKOLA ESTÉS, PH.D., AUTHOR OF* WOMEN WHO RUN WITH THE WOLVES: MYTHS AND STORIES OF THE WILD WOMAN ARCHETYPE

The wild woman, or in essence our very own wild mother. The wild mother that gives birth to us all, and gifts us with her treasures. Oh great mother, I was coerced by the seductive, oppressive patriarchy to abandon you and the wild mother in me. In the glistening darkness, in the waters of the dreamtime, there lies a treasure. I can see it, feel it, hear it and sense it.

My intuition found me. The Tiger's treasure. And tigers aren't nice.

The forest floor feels cool
My heartbeat echoes
against the skin-like bark of the branches
I climb up against the star-lit sky
Rain dances on my back
I smell of night
I'm made of rock
dirt
roots
leaves
stripes of black and amber
I run like the pulse of the wild mother.

Windy Cook is the best-selling author of *The Sisterhood of The Mindful Goddess* and contributing author of *The New Feminine Evolutionary: Embody Presence, Become the Change.* She is also the author of Following Windy, an interactive blog for hopeful mothers struggling with fertility issues at "Moms Like Me." Windy is a graduate of the Journey of Young Women Mentoring Girls  Certificate Training and enjoys holding "Winds of Change" sacred circles for girls, mothers, and women of all ages. She also has formal training as a physio-neuro trainer, is certified in Reiki II, and is a ThetaHealing practitioner and instructor.

Windy's path includes work as a family therapist at Denver Children's Home for troubled youth and as a third-grade teacher in an inner-city public school for gifted and talented children. She holds a master's degree of Social Work from the University of Denver as well as a master's degree in Educational Psychology from the University of Colorado, Denver. She is Phi Beta Kappa from Colorado State University.

Passionate about philanthropic causes, Windy supports educational, environmental, and other nonprofit programs that promote the well-being of women and children. Windy can be found in a nearby yoga studio, hiking, playing with her children, picking sage, walking her dog, or riding her bike in open space. She lives in Colorado with her beloved husband, three children, and golden retriever. Learn more at **www.windflowercook.com.**

Reclaiming Our Bodies as Sacred Sovereign Ground

BY LAINIE LOVE DALBY

> "When you feed yourself that which truly
> nourishes you, wisely and generously, you
> shall become one who can also feed the
> world that for which it truly hungers."
>
> —*ALANA FAIRCHILD*

I was still wet with shower dew, my brown and blonde locks hanging heavy and dripping over my left shoulder. My eyes downcast, I had to look away. My heart started sinking with despair to see the numbers were creeping upward, *still*. 2-5-9 stared back at me in bright red from the cheap plastic scale (my own personal torture device). At only five foot two inches, the excess weight was really starting to take its toll on my small frame.

I walked over to the mirror and let my beige XL towel drop to the floor with a thud. There I was, fully nude and vulnerable with splotchy red patches dotting my body from the water's intense cleansing heat. I hadn't been able to look at myself in the mirror in months, avoiding it at all costs. But staring at my shape in the glass in that moment, I tried desperately to conjure up a sense of kindness for the woman staring back at me.

Instead, I found myself cringing, desperate, and cruel.

All the voices that had shamed and berated me over the years arose in that moment like a vengeful symphony: *"You're too fat. You need to lose some weight. You should really cover yourself up. What's wrong with you? You're a loser. You can't control yourself. You pig..."*

I started to shake and quiver, tear buds forming at the corners of my eyes. My jaw tightened and I bit my lip until I tasted iron. Blood oozed while the familiar feeling of deep hatred, rage, and frustration emerged from deep within. My own thoughts screamed back in response, *Why me? Why did I have to get this body? Am I being punished? I hate you! This just isn't fair!!?*

I felt like I'd been sentenced to a lifetime of imprisonment in a body I didn't want and might not ever be able to love.

Hatred. The exact opposite of love and reverence.

It always started there.

You see, Beloved, I grew up as an obese, creative outcast and, my spirit was squashed relentlessly through violence and bullying from the world around me, the dieting industry and even my own family. People couldn't handle my big, wild energy, free creative spirit and blinding bright light, so they tried to dampen it. I eventually internalized this violence and over the years turned it against myself, gaining and losing over 1,300 pounds through yo-yo dieting, various eating disorders, unhealthy addictions, and self-hatred. Deeply disconnected from what matters most, my soul was starving: for meaning, purpose, direction, and wholeness. I didn't know how it felt to be truly *full*. I was awake yet sleepwalking through my days, filled with the urge to stuff and placate my deep longing for something more.

In short, I had learned to distrust and disconnect from my own body and inner soul voice, shutting down my free spirit and going into autopilot. I had become a prisoner of the patriarchal social paradigm, a slave to a culture that assaults the body. As author and filmmaker Sharron Rose has wondered, "What kind of diseased culture endorses a cult of self-starvation, self-mutilation, and hysteria in its women?" Sadly, this American life.

I hadn't been taught about the miraculous power of my unique feminine form. No one shared the ancient wisdom of the Moon mysteries around the kitchen table, the magic of blood rites and our connection to the Ocean's tides or the general field of wonder that our body is. I hadn't been told that we are radical creators with every breath, able to focus our life force energies and intentions into manifesting all we desire. I didn't learn in history class or in vacation Bible school about the Goddess as primordial Creatrix, modeling the empowering divine feminine principle of cosmic creation and ability to give birth to all new life. This deep and essential wisdom has all been long suppressed...and to our great detriment.

Instead of celebrating our inherent power and claiming our sovereignty, we are living in a time of deep soul loss. We have an epidemic of individuals today disconnected from their bodies and their essence, being repressed from reaching their full (r)evolutionary potential by patriarchal structures such as the dieting industry, fashion magazine culture, and the media— keeping them weak and stuck in a feedback loop of *"I'm not good enough, attractive enough, thin enough, strong enough to do, x, y, z (insert here: start that business, find true love, write my book, follow my dreams...)."* I know because I was one of those disconnected souls.

I didn't realize then that these systems—especially the dieting industry—are overt and covert forms of violence against women, girls, and anyone else who doesn't fit the mold of what the status quo expects regarding shape, size, skin color, or gender expression.

Patriarchal society has created unattainable success markers and images of "beauty" to keep us occupied and repressed, and like the dutiful dieting daughter I was raised to be, I was always so busy focusing on the next weight loss fad that I completely ignored listening to my own innate rhythms. I was so caught up in the number on the scale that I failed to tap into the sacred wisdom of my body and her subtle communications.

This was all before I understood my body's secret soulful language, her ethereal dance of intuition...before I reclaimed her as sacred and holy sovereign ground. It wasn't until a four-year illness careened unexpectedly into my life that I had no other choice but to walk through the fires of transmutation and *wake up.* That's when walking the path of the body truly called to me—but more on that soon, Beloved.

Heartbreakingly, I know my story isn't unique. Collectively, we have had our life force squandered through the systemic controlling, devaluing, suppression, and disavowal of women, people of color, indigenous people, LGBTQIA people, disabled people, and other marginalized individuals, and the Earth itself in our patriarchal culture. From rape and bullying to deforestation and fracking, our sacredness has been stomped on and snuffed out. (Think about it: rape and fracking are the same thing, just one is forcibly penetrating the human body and the other the body of the Earth.)

It is precisely because of this systematic oppression that we in the West have become severely malnourished, with obese bodies and starving souls.

Because of this we have lost our attunement with both Mother Nature and our own inner natures, which has led to escalating rates of depression, low self-esteem, and an overall lack of self-worth. I know how all too common this is from the thousands of women and LGBTQIA individuals that I've mentored over the years in my spiritual and leadership development practice. Deeply embedded in our culture is a harmful narrative that teaches us to hate and doubt ourselves instead of encouraging us to know that we are precious Divine Beings possessing unique medicine that's needed now. Because of this, countless individuals are hiding their light and deepest gifts—because they're waiting on the weight, or the right partner, or the perfect wardrobe, or to be given permission—wasting valuable energy and creativity that could be used to serve the greater good. Is the obsession with a "thigh gap," for instance, really a "thought gap," or a momentary lapse in consciousness that would make someone even think about something so inconsequential? But this is where we largely find ourselves now, Beloved. It's time we wake up to the insidious manipulation of our minds, bodies, hearts, and souls.

Imagine if even ten percent of the time that we spend thinking about our bodies, weight, and external appearance was redirected toward solutions for healing our world? What a difference that would make.

For me, the greatest gift of this journey of awakening was an enormous paradigm shift: I opted to ditch dieting for the Divine and focus on deep nourishment instead. I even banned the word "*die*ting" from my vocabulary. (First of all it has the word *die* in it. I'm here to sustain *life*, thank you very much!) This reframe allowed me to turn my inner fierce feminine fire and life force into a productive renewable energy source to help heal myself and the world through my sacred work. Because, when that life force is not channeled or allowed its full expression, it turns into depression or anxiety.

I also realized that, for me specifically, the excess weight was a cry for help to point out an imbalance in my life and health. **I learned that fat isn't something to be feared. It's a gift.** It was a direct communication from my body trying to say *"Hey! Something is out of balance, Beloved. Let's see what we can do about it in partnership to restore you to peak vitality and life force."* It was a plea to help me turn inward to find my own truth and wellness. And, tuning within was a salvation from the noise and static of the outside world telling me who I should be, what I should look like, how I was supposed to eat, how much I was supposed to weigh, how often I should exercise, how I should behave, what I should wear...

There is clearly a sickness of our wildness today, a deep suppression and vilification of the Divine and Fierce Feminine as well as the darkness. The predominant systems are continually trying to sterilize and tame that which is primal, messy, wild, or emerging from the pitch black womb of creation—from the literal birth process to our full range of emotions to menstruation to the forthright expression of our sacred rage. They expect us to be buttoned-up, "good girls" and rule-abiding members of society, but, instead, we are numbed out on antidepressants and pain killing opiates.

ENOUGH IS ENOUGH! It's time that we take a stand in our *SACRED NO* against the violence being perpetrated against women, girls, LGBTQIA, people of color, indigenous people, disabled people, and other marginalized individuals—and to our Mother Earth.

The world is crying out for a great homecoming now. A home-coming back to the land, our bodies, and the he(art) of what matters most...

Reconnection is the medicine that is most greatly needed in our world right now. Reconnection to our truth, our planetary family, our sacred purpose, our power, our sovereignty, and our great sentient Mother Earth to avert the ecological crisis upon us. For I am Her and She is me. We are of the Earth, inextricably entwined with Gaia. It's time to awaken to our interconnectedness with Her and all beings, honor the spirit and Divine spark in all things, and act from a higher consciousness.

What we need is a Sacred (R)evolution™ of love and reverence for self, other, the planet and the Web of All Life.

I believe that it is this sacred reconnection that will bring an end to the rampant violence in our world, both overt and covert, and restore us to our dignity and humanity. We even need to reconnect to our shadow, since without embracing our full darkness we can't experience our full light.

It's time we re-member who we truly are and why we're here, Beloved, so we can end the cycles of abuse on ourselves, our children, and future generations to come. Let us remember that we are Divine creators, connected to original Source creativity and the Great All That Is—this cosmos filled with vast aliveness, multiple forms of intelligence, and consciousness in all things.

I invite you to take a moment of awe, gratitude, and reverence with me now for our bodies. Our hearts beat over 115,200 times per day. Just think of all the effort the heart exerts on our behalf in each moment. When do we ever take time to stop and thank our bodies for their service to our life here on earth? For the majority of us our stomachs are constantly digesting our food so we can have the nutrients we need to survive. Our ears allow in the beauty of piano, jazz and pop music to delight us. Our eyes filter in the color, beauty and wonders of our world. Our bodies are magnificent masterpieces, yet instead of acknowledging this we get stuck on the surface appearance and cutting ourselves down. And the Earth! When do we give gratitude for all She does to sustain us and support *life* on our planet?

The Earth is our original ancestor. Coming home to Her is a way to come home to our own bodies, beginning to see ourselves as a reflection of nature all around us. Our bodies are made of Earth. They are nature, one and the same. The profound beauty of the sunset is in the irises of our eyes closing at night; the grain of sand is reflected in our microscopic cells.

Would you look in the sky and say, *"Stars, I hate you! You're so ugly!"* Of course not. Even the idea of that is absolutely ridiculous. But doing that to our bodies *is the same thing*. We are that: stardust and matter in human form. Radiance is the nature of our embodiment here, our soul purpose!

Our miraculous bodies are the altar of our very Being, not the bane of our existence. *They are an elaborate cloak for our souls...*

The next time you speak unkindly to your body, I invite you to put your hand on the part of your body that you feel compelled to criticize and visualize all the organs underneath your flesh that are working so tirelessly on your behalf. Take a moment to say *"thank you"* and send them some love and gratitude. Whisper *"You are sacred"* to each in turn. If you'd like to take this even further, then I invite you to write a love letter or create some expressive art to a part of your body that you've struggled with or abused often. *Think: chin, arm skin, thighs, cellulite, butt, excess weight, body fat, stomach.*

The bottom line is that it's time that we move from violence against the body to deep loving partnership *with* the body. An essential part of that is reclaiming our bodies as sacred and holy *sovereign* ground. It's the only way we're going to heal and return to our true nature so we can Sparkle Shamelessly* for the good of all! Let us reclaim and celebrate the parts of us that have been shamed and transform our pain into a greater capacity to love. Especially if there is an ancient hatred that you desire to heal. For as the metaphysical text *A Course in Miracles* states, "The holiest place on earth is where an ancient hatred has become a present love."

Let this be a HOLY HOMECOMING, Beloved.

Because our world has become a fundamentally unhealthy place, our bodies and souls (and the Earth) are crying out to be cared for, embraced, and nourished by us on a deep level. They yearn for us to be tender, gentle, and loving, a form of mothering ourselves just as our Earth Mother cares for and sustains us. That's why "Deep Nourishment for All" is one of the core thirteen pillars of what I've deemed as the Sacred (R)evolution˚. As author and cancer thriver Kris Carr has said, "Staying well is a revolutionary act." And it is also an individual journey only you can take, Beloved. There is no one-size-fits-all answer. Tuning into your own body and discerning what is true for *you* in any and every moment is essential—having that be the barometer of truth in your life, regardless of what noise in the outside world is squawking in your ear.

Being disconnected from our inner truths and our sacred vessels in this lifetime has kept us disconnected from our power and ability to choose from a place of deep grounded truth. Let's come back home, fully into our em-body-ment, so we can be the individuals we're capable of being now... embodied leaders helping to heal the world.

Because if we're not in our bodies, we can't be in our full (r)evolutionary potential.

This was one of the biggest elements that was missing for me in the journey of offering my sacred work to the world. I was always in my leadership, but I wasn't *embodied* in my leadership. I've had a challenging time being in this body, feeling safe here and in my own skin. One of my greatest struggles has been channeling the blindingly bright sparkling cosmic dancing firestar Being that I am into a human form in this 3D reality. I was always dissociating from old trauma stored in my cellular memory and leaving my body, so I could go be in the visionary realm where I felt most comfortable. It's been a continual journey to come back, to return, to spiral back into my earth suit and ground into Gaia. To ultimately welcome myself back home again and again. That's why I'm sharing this journey with you now, Beloved. In hopes that it may ease your own path.

*The healing (r)evolution and road to deep nourishment truly
began for me with the call to "Purify the Vessel." I ask, what
might be calling you, Beloved?*

The message kept coming for years (in meditations, walking in the woods, in my Dreamtime, on the train) yet I didn't know what it meant. I tried drinking green juice, working out, and eating better, but the truth is that I didn't know the first thing about how to nourish myself in this world filled with plastic food, GMOs, chemical-laden nutrients, fast food, and vast amounts of conflicting knowledge in the field of "nutrition." So I went on a personal deep dive to learn what my body needed to be sustained. I also began to ask for guidance and pray for a release of all that no longer served me so I could step fully into my spiritual leadership in the world.

This is when everything changed and I truly learned to be careful what you pray for...

What I received as an "answer" forever changed my life and sent me on a journey of surrender and awakening: a four-year illness became my alchemical cauldron and crucible of shamanic initiation. Where I was truly able to turn the lead into gold and the darkness into the dawn, and to start Sparkling Shamelessly in the world once again as an emissary of light, holding a higher frequency and vibration.

Though this was a comprehensive, multi-layered healing process that I go into more deeply in my forthcoming book, *The Great Homecoming*, here I want to bring forward a few short insights along the journey that were essential to my own healing, growth, and metamorphosis. Beloved, may these Sacred Seven inspire your own holy homecoming and reclamation of your body as sacred sovereign ground.

1. SLOWING DOWN

Early on I was drawn to work with animal medicine like my ancient Druid ancestors. Turtle was my original guide for this journey of learning how to truly slow down, to feel comfortable in my own skin, and to take my home with me wherever I went to feel safe and protected. I had to step out of the momentum tunnel of life and into greater spaciousness. I was guided during this time to turn within, reflect, and engage in deep rest and restoration from our fast-paced technological society. I regularly turned off my devices, social media, the news and especially all TV. **I needed to unhook from mass consciousness**. Instead I came into *stillness* through breathwork and other modalities to enter into full presence for the journey that was unfolding. This allowed me to shift from surface existence to the subtle realm of my soul voice so that I could stay close to it in all I do. Ultimately, turtle taught me what I like to call *soul-care*.

2. PURIFYING

In the spaciousness, I was able to release and let go of all that no longer served me, from plastic Tupperware and chemical cleaners to bleach-filled menstrual pads, from toxic foods packed with sugar and other poisons to old energetic skins and memorabilia laden with negative memories. I shed it all like a snake sheds its skin and began to purify my vessel for the journey as I had been originally called to do. **I thought of it as renovating my soul's address for greater well-being and aliveness.** To heal my physical body through food, all roads led me to Paleo, so I eventually developed my own way of eating that was close to the Earth and part of the greater homecoming. It's essentially like the well known Whole 30 protocol but with my own *sacred* twist, or what I like to think of as Shamanic Nourishment focusing in on the spiritual aspect of food. As Hippocrates said so long ago, "Let food be thy medicine and medicine be thy food." This was—and still is—a mantra for me. It wasn't about weight loss in any moment, even though I easefully shed more than 100 pounds for the first time in my life. It was all about purifying my sacred vessel for the Divine to pour through and inhabiting my aliveness fully while here on earth. It was a great release so I could live fully into my divine legacy and life purpose. I got out of my own way and became the hollow bone that Spirit blows through, the living chalice of love spilling over into the world. I also released any attachment to the number on the scale and my preconceived notions of beauty, allowing my true nature and form to emerge organically and come into balance.

3. RECONNECTING

Once my channel was clearer, I was able to tune into the wisdom of the body and hear her subtle language all the more through consistent spiritual practice. Intuitive movement, free dancing, Qoya movement (I even became a certified Qoya teacher!), and labyrinths were powerful tools for me to come back into my vessel along with other embodied somatic practices that helped me to drop down from my head into my heart and a greater sense of compassion for myself and our world. As the Native proverb shares, "The longest journey you'll ever make is the 18 inches from your head to your heart." I also spent time in ritual and ceremony connecting with the unseen realms and my ancestors for support, as well as tapping into the spirits of the land. Even though I live in the concrete jungle of New York City, I began to spend more time on the Earth as well, "Earthing" with my bare feet in the soil and laying my full body down on the land to help lower my inflammation and restore balance to my body. I began to experiment with herbal remedies, choosing to lean into Earth's gentle wisdom rather than the blunt and indiscriminate approach of the pharmaceutical industry. I started to make gratitude offerings to Her as well, including my menstrual blood. I became intimately familiar with my main spirit animals that travel with me, connecting more with the Tree and Stone People (aka crystals) and learning to experience all living Beings as my brothers, sisters, and Beloveds—even the Stars. Working with the Celtic Wheel of the year, Goddess wisdom, and ancient women's ways also helped me to reconnect with my own Earth-based indigenous heritage of Celtic Shamanism, Druidry, and Paganism. Overall, **I literally needed to root into the Earth to rise into my full power and (r)evolutionary potential.**

4. LISTENING

I was returning more each day back home to myself, to the quiet voice within my own heart, which led me to connect with the inner knowing of my body's inherent rhythms and cycles. I needed to honor the ache to tap into the mystery of life as well as the sacred pulse of ancient wisdom within my own body. I began tracking my body with the help of Lucy Pearce's *Full Circle Health* book, noting how I was feeling, where I was in my moon cycle, and what was happening with the heavenly bodies in the sky via astrology, knowing that each was affecting me on a profound level. It was a process of beginning to see my body as an accountability buddy instead of an enemy, one who has my back and is just trying to communicate with me in the only ways she knows how—with aches and pains, vertigo, strange ringing in my ears—all just to say, *"Hello! Something is out of balance!"* With this process of deep listening, as well as the help of an integrative doctor, my spiritual counselor, and a healer who used muscle testing, I was also able to begin learning and understanding the miraculous foreign language of my body. Instead of using the old masculine model of abusing my body and trying to control it by beating myself up at the gym, trying to 'top down' weight loss, I instead shifted to a feminine model of receiving and opening to inner wisdom, guidance, and intuition to do what felt good in my body, opting for ease and flow. This helped me to learn just how sensitive my body truly is and how I'd been bulldozing her for years, which in turn led to some very necessary self-forgiveness work.

5. DISCERNING

Hummingbird was my main inspiration for this part of the journey in learning fierce discernment and getting to know my own *sacred no* and *holy hell yes* feel in my body. That's where I always find the core truths. Deep within. Hummingbirds are incredible creatures that memorize thousands of flowers and only go back to the ones that nourish them the most. They seek out the sweetness and return, again and again. They also have the largest hearts of any living being based on their overall size, necessary for the extraordinary journeys they take. (It's also why they are a main feature of my shamanic healing artwork on the cover of the this book!) Each day I practice refocusing my attention and life force energies on the he(art) of what matters most in order for me to fully honor my body temple and my sacred work in the world. "Dancing for Discernment" is also one of my favorite practices I developed to help determine which path is best for me. It's discernment through *feeling* instead of *thinking*. It drops me straight into my body and her powerful sacred wisdom every time.

6. NOURISHING

Along the way I learned that nourishment isn't just about food, it's about overall sustenance for holistic thriving—womb-level nourishment at the deepest level of my Being. Because what you eat, what you drink, what you think, who you surround yourself with, and what you put into your body *matters*—physically, energetically, and otherwise. Where we put our life force energies, and how we show up in the world with our unique medicine and deep gifts *matters*. If we're not nourished, we're not able to access our full life force energies and creative capacities in service to the greater good. I also learned that **if we're not nourished, we can't nourish the world with our sacred work.** I discovered that one of the core ways that I'm deeply nourished is by coming together in Beloved Community and sacred sisterhood circles to do ritual and ceremony to heal, play, grow, and transform into our full (r)evolutionary potential together. I saw that we are complicit in each other's healing and the greater healing of the world at this time. We are here to serve as intricate mirrors for each other's greatness and brilliant light. The truth is that we are stronger together, amplifying our energy and social impact through mutual support. *I ask you now: What nourishment does your body need to* thrive, *Beloved?*

7. SERVING

We are not hungry for what we're not getting; we are hungry for what we're not giving. I deeply believe that each and every one of us has a precious human life. We *matter* and we're each here to *do* something that matters. What we say, think, and create makes a difference. Each one of us is needed *now* to show up in the fullness of who we truly are. We each have a unique medicine and what I like to call #SOULSPARKLE that only we can bring. If we don't add it to the great cosmic masterpiece, it will be lost forever. We are living in a time of global crisis. It's time we come out of hiding fully and step up in service to the greater good.

I invite you to try any or all of the practices above that feel resonant for you, Beloved. That's most important—that it feels true for you in *your* body. Because this journey of healing and becoming whole is about stripping away all the constraints that society, family, and others have put on us in order to come back to our bodies' own indigenous roots so we can discover what will best serve us, our vessels, and our life. It's making a choice to no longer accept the rules as they're given, especially from the dieting industry and patriarchal systems of oppression, and instead reinvent them so our own bodies, hearts, and souls can finally *thrive*. Ultimately, it's a journey to reclaim our own inherent Divinity and live from a place of deep inner alignment to heal ourselves and our ailing world.

My prayer is that we move towards Sacred (R)evolution™ on the individual and collective level, Beloved, helping to make LOVE the new bottom line. Most of all, let us be deeply nourished now so that we can deeply nourish the world. And so it is.

Lainie Love Dalby is an embodied leadership mentor, trailblazer of women's spirituality and empowerment, holy ceremonialist, transformational speaker and retreat facilitator, published author, visionary shamanic healing artist, deep wisdom walker and blazing brave He(art) Warrior. She's on a mission to free human spirits that have been oppressed and devalued to Sparkle SHAMELESSLY® and step into their authentic power. As a spiritual thought leader with her own brand of multi-

PHOTO BY JASON MEERT

media ministry, she is using daring style, deep substance and Divine #SOULSPARKLE to dismantle old systems, ideas, and ways of being that promote separateness and limit our full (r)evolutionary potential.

She is also deeply passionate about ending the violence we perpetrate against each other and our own bodies by reminding us of our inherent divinity within and helping to bring the Sacred Feminine back into balance in our own lives and the world—in a great return to love and reverence for self, other, our planet and the great Web of All Life. To this end, she is the founder of SISTERHIVE® and the Sacred (R)evolution™ where she gathers women and the LGBTQIA community in both live and virtual sacred circles to facilitate deep healing, sacred play, soul growth, and alchemical transformation through her global community and signature immersion experiences like Ignite the Fierce Feminine Within, Sovereign Sisters Rising Initiation into the Fierce and Sacred Feminine, international retreats, and other sisterhood initiatives.

Like a modern-day medicine woman, her ultimate goal is to help us feel more comfortable in our own skin and remember who we truly are and why we're here at this most powerful time in human history by unleashing our bold creativity, innate wildness, and fierce feminine courage. She believes that TOGETHER we can co-create our lives as a great Masterpiece for the good of all and dream a new world into being. Embark on the journey with her free Sacred (R)evolution™ Starter Kit at **www.lainielovedalby.com** and on Instagram **@LainieLoveDalby.**

Special Gift

Join the Sacred (R)evolution™!
Get your FREE Sacred (R)evolution™ Starter Kit at
www.lainielovedalby.com

And for all women-identified individuals, get a free month
trial in our SISTERHIVE® global community. Come receive
monthly sustained DEEP NOURISHMENT for your mind,
body, heart, and SOUL!
Visit **http://bit.ly/sisterhive** and use the coupon
code SACREDBODY.

Voices In The Moonlight

BY AURORA FARBER

"When the night has come
And the land is dark
And the moon is the only light we'll see
No I won't be afraid
No I won't be afraid
Just as long as you stand, stand by me"

"STAND BY ME" SONG LYRICS
BY BEN E. KING, JERRY LEIBER AND MIKE STOLLER

The dark night, the dark land, the moon...the only light I see. I feel a visceral remembrance of despair as I hear this song...but my lyrics were different then. I felt abandoned and afraid. No, terrified. With my world spinning out of control, I collapsed onto the bed and dared to whisper the word that led me into this deep, mysterious darkness..."melanoma".

This wasn't my first cancer scare. Two years earlier, I discovered a breast lump that catalyzed a desperate need to care for my body and claim my life. Wanting some kind of control over the threat of cancer, I radically changed my diet, lost 20 pounds, and became a fierce advocate for my own healthcare choices. With determination and ferocity, I was dedicated to beat this my way and sought alternative treatments to bring my body back to wholeness again.

And yet...after all that, cancer found me, hiding from sight in a mole on my back. The mole was quickly removed, but not forgotten and I held on to this betrayal with a fierce tenacity that left me numb, sad, broken, and frozen.

Lost in the fear of death and feelings of betrayal, I disconnected from my body even as I attended the routine appointments to check my skin, eyes, and mouth for cancer with both diligence and dread. At home, I walked through everyday moments in a frozen numbness, too afraid to feel, too scared to slip into the darkness once more. My robotic mantra was "Wake up. Tidy the house. Help the kids with homework. Cook. Bathe. Sleep. Repeat."

My body became a "vessel of doing," no longer the "vessel of my being." I was petrified to inhabit her intimately again. I didn't trust her. What if she let me down again?

With indignance I thought, "My body did not 'stand by me' through the great changes I had made to honor her. Why should I bother to connect with her now?" With every passing day I fortified the disconnection between my body and spirit, laying another brick of resentment down so I could wall her off completely.

It was surprisingly easy to do, and so *familiar*. This disconnection had begun long ago. It was only during this crisis, when my body wasn't "performing" as I commanded, that I saw the cost of the years of my own betrayal which came in the form of neglect, silence, judgment, denial, and comparison.

For years I had listened to voices outside myself, trying desperately to shape myself and my body into someone, *something* acceptable enough to be worthy of love.

External voices holding me to standards of beauty, appropriateness, and perfection.

Cultural voices telling me to be smart, pretty, polite, kind and put everyone else's needs first.

Comparative voices guiding me to a false feminine standard of being thin and soft-spoken, yet assertive and even sexy, but never *too* sensual, especially in owning my own pleasure.

Prescriptive voices that told me the "right" way to diet, exercise, what to eat, how much water to drink, and how much sleep I needed in a one-size-fits-all kind of way.

These voices clamoring around in my head sometimes screaming, sometimes whispering...

Get busy
Stop dreaming
Hurry up
Be more
Buy more
Achieve more
You're so slow
You're too fat
You're too skinny
You're so lazy
You're too ambitious
You're too assertive
You're too sexy
You're too wild
You're too much
Calm down
Do it this way
Do it my way
Be different
Act your age
Grow up
Take this
Fix that
Just listen to me
Listen to them
Listen to anyone but yourself
You don't know anything
You think you know everything
Just stop it
Just do it
Just do something
Just change
Because right now
You're just not enough
And probably never will be

These voices crippled me, overpowering and shutting down the one voice that really mattered. The voice of my own essence longing to call me home; longing to be sung and danced through this body; longing to *stand by me* though the darkness and into the moonlight.

AN AWAKENING, A RE-MEMBRANCE

I stayed stuck in numbness for months, until the passionate rhythm of a Spanish love song activated my reawakening. Listening to the music, my body responded and my hips began to move. Snaking itself up my spine, this rhythm unlocked something in my heart, then throat and finally my eyes, as lyrics of heartbreak, betrayal, and anger mixed with a deep longing for love.

Crying and shaking, I sang and danced this love song to my body. Anger, betrayal, guilt, and shame burned within my heart's violet flame of compassion and forgiveness, as years of my own neglect, expectation, and judgment washed away in a river of tears.

My hair wild, my face wet, my body shaken, raw and alive again, I fell to the floor...rocking and consoling her, *my sacred body,* sharing my deepest heartfelt love for *her.*

Awakened, I remembered. I re-membered my body for who she is... vessel of my BEing, my essence, temple of my spirit. My beloved body, *standing by me through ALL of it.* Never betraying me. Never neglecting me. Never. Ever. Forgetting me.

I vowed to rebuild my relationship with her, not out of fear or desperation, but devotion. I began each day in gratitude for my beloved body temple. With a heart of devotion, I tended her with oils and fragrant baths by candlelight; with quiet reflection, journaling and gratitude practices; with light, love and laughter as I began to connect with others again; with colorful clothing and crystal jewelry to help me embody the passionate, vibrant and whole woman I knew still lived within.

Still cautious of the sun, I sought sanctuary in nature only at night, and noticed how the moon started as a tiny sliver, grew into fullness, only to shrink back into the darkness once more. Each night as I witnessed the shifting cadence, I sensed the emergence of a new feminine wisdom path, the changing moonlight giving me hope of a harmonious, joyful, *feminine* way of being.

I realized that the disconnection with my body had come from listening to the external voices of a hurried, expectant world with distorted masculine standards. For years I had strived to be perfect, bright, and fixed like the sun, following a 24-hour cycle of waking and working, and only resting when my body collapsed into sleep at night.

The moon phases gave me a new rhythm to follow, a waxing and waning energy that was feminine, cyclical and regenerative. By following the moon cycle, I began to feel my own energy waxing and waning, lighting up an unexpected, magical inner moon within. This *moon of my womb* was tied to my menstrual cycle and had been laying a trail of moonlight for me to follow since my teenage years.

Intuitively, I knew that reclaiming this inner moon would help me navigate the world on my own terms, illuminating an ancient path to "reset, recharge, renew and reflect" each quarter phase while being lovingly held by the magic of the moon.

MOON MAGIC

The moon brought me new powerful insights on how to live a more harmonious life. This was an ancient wisdom path that women had been following for years. Before our modern world, women gathered in "red tents" to honor their moon cycles, "mothering" themselves and one another...sharing stories, braiding each other's hair, passing on the wisdom teachings from mother to daughter. This "time in" nurtured the body, mind and spirit, nourishing the energy that would be needed later as the moon grew into fullness.

Our ancient sisters knew the power of the moon to pull the tides of the great oceans, and its power to pull the tides of our own energy and power. They recognized that our bodies are not built to always spend "time out" in the world. We need "time in" too, sacred time to shrink back into ourselves, to find ourselves, so that we can bloom again. Watching the phases of the moon, they understood that women are always changing, growing into fullness and turning inwards again...guided by their inner moon compass, syncing it in a cosmic rhythm to the great orb in the sky.

As I embraced this ancient wisdom, a new vibrancy and sense of a gratitude emerged. I began to dream again, to let go of the fear of dying, to appreciate each day as a gift. This connection between my inner moon and the moon above helped me deepen my connection to my body and to Mother Earth. I felt the embodied knowing that I was divinely supported and cosmically held.

THE MOON PHASE ARCHETYPES

Hungry for more moon wisdom, I deepened my commitment to align my feminine energy with the moon and became a Priestess Initiate of the 13 Moon Mystery School, an Avalonian mystery school founded by Ariel Spilsbury. The 13 divine feminine archetypes gave me new models of feminine power, love and wisdom, inviting me to an expression of myself that was larger than I ever imagined.

Each moon cycle I felt more supported and held by these archetypes and their ties to both the yearly seasons and to my menstrual cycle. By looking into the night sky, I navigated my life with these energies by seeding, sprouting, blooming and harvesting each moon cycle...then letting it all go so I could begin again. This regenerative cycle nourished me deeply, helping me face the shadows of "not enoughness" that I had carried and reinforced for decades. As my inner light began to shine again, I found moonlight in the shadows, even in this fearful journey with cancer. I realized I was given melanoma, a sun cancer, so that I would embrace the darkness and discover the magic of my own divinely feminine rhythm reflected in the moonlight.

Since then, I've lived my life in alliance with the moon. The moon's cadence allowing me time to alchemize my shadows; the moonlight, illuminating my own gifts, strengths and talents. Each cycle an opportunity to die and be reborn again and again. Each quarter phase offering me a new feminine voice as a guide. Instead of judgment, comparison and shame, I hear words of comfort, support, pleasure and wisdom. These four feminine faces of the moon, born from my adversity to become my allies and guides... Mother...Queen...Goddess...Sage.

Voices of my inner archetypes guiding me to a new, wholistic, holographic way of being. Voices activating my true voice in devotion to my own divine feminine awakening.

AT THE NEW MOON

Be a Mother to Your Body

Beloved, precious one
You are loved no matter what.
I am here for you always, all ways.
In the darkness, there is a new beginning.
Feel my arms around you,
Soothing you,
Holding you,
Supporting you.
Rest, relax and be renewed.
Forgive the past and begin afresh.
Open your intuition and receive my gifts.
Plant your heart intentions for this new beginning
Each cycle, a chance of renewal;
Each ending, a new beginning.
You are precious, beloved,
Like a baby I hold in arms.
I will always love you.

On this new moon
Cradle yourself in your own arms and
Love like a mother

AT THE 1ST QUARTER MOON

Be the Queen of Your Queendom

Hail and welcome royal one!
Sovereign being
Powerful, full of integrity and purpose.
As the moon waxes, feel your growing power.
Look at the world you are creating...your Queendom.
See it's many facets...body, mind, spirit,
Your family, your sacred work
The temple of your home and your body.
With a heart of gratitude, use your discernment
To see where you are out of integrity with your desires.
Take full responsibility for your life
Activate your innate power as a Queen and Creatrix
To break free from limiting beliefs
And water the seeds of the intentions that are sprouting.
Sovereign one,
Balanced in your masculine and feminine power,

At this 1st Quarter Moon,
Empower your dreams and
Take inspired action as you
Reign like a Queen

AT THE FULL MOON

Be a Goddess of Love and Light

Radiant Goddess,
Open up your senses to the fullness of the moon
And your innate grace, beauty, and pleasure.
It's time to descend the throne
To walk barefoot on the earth.
Dare to howl and dance in fearless passion and
Celebration of the fullness of your life.
This is your time to be embodied in gratitude!
Sense the air on your skin.
Anoint yourself with essential oils.
Take scented bubble baths by candlelight.
Turn yourself on with pleasure and
Feel the nourishment that pleasure brings.
Let it crack you open in gratitude
As you share yourself authentically
With raw, untamed, open-hearted presence.
Dare to shine in the moonlight
And open your heart
To give and receive.

On this full moon, sensual beauty
Evoke the divine
In yourself and others as you
Shine like a Goddess

AT THE 3RD QUARTER MOON

Harvest and Share Your Sage Wisdom

Wise One, the third quarter moon brings the final harvest.
A time of completion, getting things done
Simplifying and releasing.
Make space in your life for reflection,
It's time to go within again.
Clear the fields so that they can lie dormant once more.
Enjoy the harvest of the wisdom you've gathered
Through the challenges and initiations
With delight and gratitude.
Write, sing, dance, paint, plant it.
Share it with others
And then let it all go.
Release. Shed. Surrender.
Fall into the arms of the freedom of the unknown
Where limitless possibilities await.
What mythic story will you create this next cycle
As you seed, sprout, bloom, and harvest
With the moon cycle?
What mythic imprint will be the eternal mark
Of your life and legacy of love?

On this 3rd quarter moon
Harvest your wisdom
And lead like a Sage

Unlimited possibility awaits us in the magic of the moonlight. Each year, each month, each day, patriarchal voices of judgment are vanquished by these four feminine faces of the moon, gently rocking us in her rhythmic embrace.

In the shifting moonlight, a magnificent chorus of feminine voices sing us home...guiding us to a new, divinely feminine way of being as we choose to re-member ourselves by the light of the moon...

Love like a Mother
Reign like a Queen
Shine like a Goddess
Lead like a Sage

Aurora Anurca Farber, Women's Leadership Coach, Writer, Speaker and modern-day Priestess, is on a mission to help women ignite their "Feminine Fire" the 3 flames of POWER, LOVE and WISDOM that are the key to awakening the new feminine evolutionary conscious-ness that will heal our world. She helps women burn away limiting beliefs, align with their feminine moon rhythm, and embody their mythic purpose in the world.

Aurora holds honors degrees in Literature and Foreign Language, along with a professional certification in Coaching. She is a co-author of three books in the The New Feminine Evolutionary series published by Flower of Life Press: *The New Feminine Evolutionary: Embody Presence, Become the Change; Pioneering the Path to Prosperity: Discover the Power True Wealth and Abundance;* and *Sacred Body Wisdom: Igniting the Flame of Our Divine Humanity.*

Through private coaching, online programs, women's circles, and retreats, Aurora creates "sacred spaces" for women to be held, wit-nessed, and loved exactly as they are right here, right now. Her guiding vision is a world of women claiming their creative powers, loving their body temples, and being beacons of fierce wisdom as they burn away archaic, limiting beliefs and light the world on fire with love. Learn more at **www.aurorafarber.com.**

Special Gift

Mythic Moon Map and Planner: Create A Mythic Life and
Find Your Feminine Flow With The Moon Cycle
Download at **www.aurorafarber.com/moon-map**

Rewrite your story and design a mythic life each moon cycle
with this one page moon-ly planner. These four moon phases
and four feminine archetypes will help you identify and "Mother"
your seed intentions; focus like a "Queen" on what is sprouting,
lovingly tend what blooms like a "Goddess," and harvest your
"Sage" wisdom/seeds for the next moon cycle.

Planting the Seeds of Returning Home

BY ELISHA HALPIN

THE DISCONNECT

Our disconnect from our body, no matter how we get there, is a consequence, a byproduct of the collective's abandonment and denial of the Divine Feminine. This is not just about female bodies. Or queer and othered bodies. Or indigenous bodies. But all bodies, including the body of the earth. When we abandoned the Divine Feminine we forgot who we truly were as humans and as souls. I don't believe this abandonment is accidental. It is this that leads each of us into our individual disconnects. The disconnect from our bodies, our tribes and communities, and our [home]lands. Isolation and scarcity are some of the fruits of the abandonment and denial of the Divine Feminine. Self-loathing, foundational beliefs of wrongness, or willingness to accept lies such as original sin are the programming that prevails.

The process of embodiment is one of coming home to ourselves through our bodies. I believe the point of life is to learn how to allow the soul to make herself home in this physical temple. So yes, this body matters. And yes, it is sacred. This process is one of remembering, reconnecting, and returning.

MY JOURNEY INTO AND THROUGH THE DISCONNECT

I was the tiny goddess covered in mud and rolling through the grass. Crossing the fields of cotton and tobacco to find the wild boars and then goad them into a chase. I was the wild little girl who would run, scream, and twirl her way up and down the hill because there was nothing more blissful than feeling myself move. I was at home. Confident. I loved being me. Being my body. I felt beautiful with shirts covered in streaks of peanut butter and jelly, with frizzy hair, and no name shoes.

Then I realized that my skin was covered with spots. That I didn't look or act like other people. I was loud and wild and opinionated. But what people focused on was how different I looked. This realization of how different I must be came through others pointing out my freckles. Even at age five I read the subtext that I was less because of them, because I looked [and was] different. But it was the difference of my body that people could pinpoint and easily name. The ridicule and being singled out for looking and being different started young. I didn't understand why it hurt. I hated the burden of being the mixed kid. I just wanted straight blond hair and creamy peach skin. Because then life would be perfect, and I would be good and beautiful.

Since I couldn't be blond and peachy, I channeled my shame at being different, the script for being less, into becoming the best. I excelled as a dancer, baton twirler, and cheerleader. I contorted my body and learned to spring into the air to please the teacher. I was physically gifted and could mold my body into whatever the next challenge needed her to be. I was dancing pre-professionally by the age of ten, having been on scholarship at the ballet academy for several years. I was committed to my future of artistic dominance over my physical form. I would transcend my not enoughness by mastering my body through beauty and art.

Unfortunately, the beauty was only in the appearance. Not in feeling and definitely not in knowing. I could make beautiful things and do amazing things with my body. But inside I felt hollow. I was a shell of a person—disconnected and disassociated from the sensorial inhabiting of this life. In fact if it wasn't going to aid in my dominance and mastery over the body, I had no interest in it. I was only as good and worthy as my body was mastered and skilled. That beautiful wild child who thought she could fly...she had clipped her wings to fit in and strive for worthiness.

Through my highly proficient and nuanced mind-body connection I was able to outsmart my hunger, best my pain, and push my body well beyond a limit I had never understood. A torn muscle or sprained ligament was the punishment I deserved for not being good enough. It was the well earned battle scars for being a warrior against the body, against feelings, against my lack as a girl.

Mastery over my body in pursuit of artistic beauty became the way I domesticated, denounced, and desensitized myself. The wild tiny goddess, now prim and proper in pink tights and black leos spent her time being the play doll of patriarchy. Ballet is an art built upon the power of the male gaze and it preys upon young women who do not understand the price we pay, for dancing on our toes is not in blood and blisters but in trading our sensual soul for applause. I was totally on board. The control and manipulation of my body made me feel my life was purposeful, that I was developing my talents as a way of proving my worthiness to be in this life. What began as a passion for movement transcended into a way of keeping sensations masked. I abandoned my body and my soul to achieve someone else's definition of success. Essentially, I handed over the keys to my castle and left the jewels out to be looted.

It wasn't until college that I had a glimpse of that free wild goddess who I was born as. Having left ballet not being able to cope with the external abuse (I was still cool with the self abuse), I began to improvise as part of my modern dance training. It was the struggle of a lifetime. Disconnection and control are not the makings of an improviser. And as much as I hated those moments in class I knew somewhere deep that it was important step for me. So I skipped the traditional dance intensive that summer and did an internship for a Theatre and Dance group all based in Improvisation. It was glorious and scary and so many seeds to returning home were planted.

It was through my journey to become an Improvisational performer, as well as with somatics, that I was forced to come face to face with myself. I learned to begin listening to my body, to follow her impulse and let her lead. I learned that the part was not greater than the whole. And throughout a decade my wholeness continued to expand as I was able to be with myself so much more. I began to feel free when I moved. Glimpses of that wild child twirling and prancing would come through. I became a fierce and dynamic performer known for being mesmerizing and fearless onstage. I began to be comfortable with the wisdom and magic of my body, but only onstage. I was not ready to take her out of the studio or off the stage. I would create my work from her insight and perceptiveness but I could not yet live that way.

It was towards the end of that decade that I re-learned to breathe (I had been holding my breath for almost twenty years at that point) and right on the heels of that I developed asthma. At the time I did not put together the significance of that timing. It is as though the more I came home to my body the more my lack of connection to life became apparent. This lack of connection to being in relationship to Life, the Universe, however we might term it, was my last big hurdle to embodiment. But big it was and it would be another half a decade before I began to dissolve that barrier.

Oh yes, that damn barrier. One of the reasons that it took another five years to find the dissolve mechanism is super important to talk about. It wasn't just *my* key to coming into true embodiment with my soul seated and at home inside this physical body—it can be your key, too.

THE RETURNING

I was standing—or more like squatting—about two thirds of the way up a mountain in the middle of Ireland. I couldn't breathe, or so I thought. Truthfully, I was not breathing well and not getting enough oxygen. If I couldn't get some air in I knew my body was heading for a shut down. Given the location of being hours from nowhere with no reliable cell coverage and with my best friend and seven year old nephew, I began to come to the realization that I might not walk back down the mountain or any mountain again. And after years of opening to sensation and coming into connection, it was this final disconnect that jolted me fully into presence and into love for this physical form. My soul wanted to come home. And as I allowed that to penetrate the darkness and the fear, I knew She could choose which home, the earthly one or the cosmic one. And it was with the sensations of love and grace of this life that flooded my physical body.

I have realized since then that so much of the numbness and fear of feeling is part of this barrier to the Divine Feminine and the reason we continue the disconnection. We carry the collective shame of being too much. We aren't shown the power of sensation. We believe this disembodiment will keep us safe, to ourselves and to others. The key then to dissolving and returning is feeling all of life.

The returning and reconnection will cost you...big time. It will cost you your addictions to things like sugar, starving, excess, gossip, and ultimately to your suffering. Releasing the disconnect will cost you your overdoing, over giving, and overwhelm. Not to mention the self-loathing, false humility, and perfectionist identify. Moving from disconnect means confronting fear as a friend and metabolizing it to get our gold from it. It means giving up the need to want to fix yourself and learning to live in your wholeness. Our disconnect from our body, from the Divine Feminine, from our soul's embodiment, will show up in every area of life. This disconnect is leading us to live with a big fat D on the report card of life. We are full of disconnect, discord, depletion, disappointment, distraction, and depression. We look everywhere but to our body for the answer.

PLANTING YOUR SEEDS

So that might all sound disheartening and overwhelming. But the truth is the path home is not as far as we think it is. So what can we do right now, today to begin our process of embodiment? What are the seeds we can plant and then cultivate as we spiral into ourselves?

Well firstly, we can stop trying to hold it together. We can plant the seed to soften and melt into ourselves. We can stop punishing ourselves for not being perfect in completing and executing. We can let go of the external and move into our Divine Feminine center.

We do this by firstly coming into acceptance around the disconnect. Acceptance is one the biggest seeds we must plant. Acceptance is not shaming. It is not blaming. It is no longer hiding or living in illusion. Acceptance is the key to ignite our transformative process. It is the element that opens the floodgates to grace.

When we can admit the disconnect from the sensations in our body, from our sensory experience, from our emotions, from our inner landscape without shaming ourselves for being where we are we can begin the alchemical process of reclaiming our gold from the shit. Planting this seed is huge and it requires that we see where we carry shame without shaming ourselves more. The seeds of compassion and forgiveness are so important, too. Falling in love with all our parts even the ones that seem wrong and broken is a major milestone in this journey home.

Our disconnect may feel like full severing right now or it may feel like some frayed edges but by landing in acceptance, upping the compassion, and choosing to love ourselves is how we can begin. Physically we do this by slowing into the breath and making space to be with ourselves right where we are. We can begin the shift into Soul/self connection.

Understanding that we have all had experiences that have led us here is important. You are not more broken than the next sister. And you do not need to be fixed. The process of healing our disconnect is one of remembering our dismembered parts and returning the expression of our wholeness.

We also must begin to plants the seeds of choice. When we remember our power to choose we can begin taking actions that are supportive and nourishing. One the best definitions of a healing journey I have ever heard is that it is learning to parent yourself. Much of our disconnect is a result of our mother (or father) wound and the carrying through her inner patriarchy which has built our inner patriarch. By learning to receive nourishment, love, support, and kindness by giving it to ourselves we begin to shift the paradigm of self-loathing and self-manipulation to execute. Love yourself into movement. Love yourself into eating the way your body needs. Love yourself into your sensual nature. Not getting the results you desire? Check that story and your intention. Are they in alignment? If yes, then just keep upping the love fest. Could this process be slower than hating yourself into a diet? Yes, sure, maybe. And so what? Why is a result worth the damage to yourself? Why is looking a certain way more important that how you feel? Why is your relationship to what others think (or you think they think) more important than having a loving trustworthy relationship with yourself?

So my final invitation is to do this 10 step embodiment practice and just begin right now to plant these seeds and cultivate the embodied presence of Divine Feminine Love.

Get comfortable. Put on something you love. Wrap in a cozy blanket. Lets stop denying comfort.

Settle in and become consciously aware of your breath. Follow the breath in and out with your mind. Feel the air moving into and out of the body. Imagine breathing in a color you love. Breathe in the state of embodiment you desire in the moment. Maybe it's calm, peace, passion, or trust. Breathe out release, letting go, and laying down the fight with yourself.

Place your hand upon your heart. Imagine a glow of pink (or any other color you want) light flowing from the palm of your hand into the center of your chest and expanding into the full chest cavity.

Feel your connection to whatever you are sitting or lying upon. Feel the floor/chair/bed rising up to hold you. Let yourself feel it. Feel the support. Let go into gravity. You don't have to hold it all up in this moment. Give yourself over to the breath, the word, and the light.

Say to yourself "I forgive you. I forgive you for EVERYTHING." Say it over and over again. Say it even if your mind is not sure that you do forgive

PLANTING THE SEEDS OF RETURNING HOME

yourself. Keep saying it while the light expands and while you breathe in your word and your color.

Begin to slowly roll your shoulders. Roll your head. Circle the foot. Wiggle your hips. Maybe lightly stretch into an arch or an arm reach.

Begin to roll and undulate the spine like a wave. Beginning at the base with the inhale and exhaling as you reach the top. Feel the sensations. Go slow. Go fast.

Shake your hands and your feet as vigorously as you can. Then move to the legs and the arms. Next the shoulders and the hips. Then the torso. Really vibrate and shake the center of the body.

Move back into being consciously aware of your breath and feeling the floor/chair/bed rising up to hold you. Gently squeeze your hands, your arms, any all parts of your body. Imagining the light from your hands moving into every part of the body.

FEEL yourself. Feel your skin and the air. Feel the sensations and movement inside the body. See yourself in your minds eye. Both the physical you and lightbody you. Feel your feelings and your emotions. Know yourself. Remember your beauty and your wholeness as your sit in your Beingness.

I love to put a beautiful song on and light a candle when I do this practice. This is a huge seed you just planted. Welcome home to your Self. She is glorious and all that you have been through with her is now a part of the journey home.

If I am disconnected from the wisdom of my body, I have abandoned my intuition. If I am disconnected, my energy is so dissipated that I am no longer a threat to the patriarchal establishment. If I stop participating in my own enslavement by being in my own body and coming into my personal power, I have just enacted a revolution. The seeds to this revolution are yours to sew, tend, and cultivate. They are the seeds to return home.

Elisha Halpin is a leader and teacher of the Divine Feminine and an empowerment mentor who works with women to uncover their innate radiance. Through 1:1, group, and immersive programs, she guides women into the process of identifying and claiming their truth. Elisha believes that through  connecting to our deep Self and embodying our Soul's unique song, we can't help but radiate light into the world.

Elisha facilitates and mentors women in their Soul healing process. Through her platform of WILDLY RADIANT she works with women to step into sovereignty through healing the past, coming fully into presence, and opening to the mystery of life. Weaving sacred magic and neuroscience together to help women make transformational changes in life, Elisha facilitates women in a rebirthing of their wild Self.

Elisha has trained in numerous modalities and frameworks, including as a Warrior Goddess Training Facilitator, Dancing Mindfulness Facilitator, Crystal Healer, Reiki and Energy Healer, and Neurosculpting Meditation Facilitator. In addition to her expertise in movement, yoga and somatics, Elisha is a professional dancer and choreographer who has performed and taught all over the world. She holds an MFA in Dance Performance and Choreography and a Certificate in Life Coaching. Whether in performance or healing, Elisha believes every moment is potent and full of magic waiting to be experienced and shared.

Learn more at **www.elishahalpin.com**; facebook: Wildly Radiant with Elisha Halpin; Instagram: @wildlyradiant_elishahalpin

Special Gift

A main component of embodiment is the process of remembering your wholeness by connecting to your Deep Self. Self-connection is one of the keys to coming home to this body. In this meditation, we ground and move into exploration of connection through sensing our light body.

ACCESS HERE: **bit.ly/elishahalpin_cominghome**

Feeding the Body of the Divine Feminine

BY SHANNON LEE NICKERSON

As a youngster, I always thought something was wrong with me—I guess you could say I was a hypochondriac. But the funny thing is, my old patterns have led me to develop a divine relationship with myself: to trust myself and to stop seeking outside of myself for answers to my own issues of health and well-being.

This goes without saying that the greatest joys in my life are my deepest and most intimate relationships with the people I love. We all need support, to feel valued, and to feel loved. But I learned at a very young age that my value and love would come from outside of myself. And that left me endlessly searching for something—turning over every stone of religion, health, spirituality, and study of the body to find a sense of peace and love for myself.

As a child, I was perfect, worthy, and loved. There was no shame or fear and certainly no unworthiness. But slowly, to fit in and be accepted, I started to give away my power. I would mimic what I saw in my teachers and family and become that. I took care of people as my mother did as a way of getting approval and love. I would righteously take a stand for myself and close my heart as my teachers did in teaching me who and what was right and wrong. Meanwhile, my body was powered by sugar and adrenaline, which left me on a never-ending path of stress and elevated cortisol levels. Ultimately, I was constantly seeking the next adrenaline high and using food for fuel—until I ran out of juice at twenty-eight years old.

Eventually, my body became my portal back into my power and into a sense of belonging with my family. I found my way back into my truth. Of course, the circumstances and relationships that followed gave me endless opportunities to reclaim my power and finally become the woman I was meant to be.

My father, a nuclear engineer, designed nuclear power plants. We moved often, and I was constantly trying to adapt to new settings and fit in at school. My home life was abundant with love and affection, but I felt powerless as my father would promise this would be the last move...and then we would move again. Moving created a life of instability. I was constantly in my head, overwhelmed, anxious, and out of control. Often I numbed these feelings with food, as I craved sugar, processed foods, and comfort foods with zero to little nutritional value.

The energy of these foods continued to feed my feelings of unworthiness, shame, and imperfection. I used food to stuff down my light, my joy... and hide the beautiful being I was inside but couldn't yet see. Macaroni and cheese, frozen pizza, Vienna sausages, frosted sugar-coated cereal packed with preservatives and artificial flavorings...The highly processed foods, and particularly the sugar, would continue to disconnect me from my spirit—my higher self. At that point, I didn't even know she existed.

I suffered from chronic allergies as a kid. I lived on Benadryl and needed antibiotics at least twice a year. My immune system would go haywire, over-reacting to everything in my environment. Strangely enough, I thought this was normal. But I was just a skinny, sick kid using food to get energy to run and play.

I grew up in a cul de sac with all boys, who were playful but rough, and I was told to toughen up. This was hard because I was sensitive. I was confused and ashamed because I cried when I couldn't take them picking on me anymore or when they played rough with me.

My dad would tell me that the boys picked on me because they were actually flirting with me. But why would they tease me and pick on me if they liked me so much? I felt shame for not being as strong as them, unable to protect myself, and confused about why this was considered flirting. More confusion—more sugar, please! This cycle continued, and I remained frustrated and disconnected from myself.

The bullying started when I was thirteen and continued well beyond high school. My high school had one sorority you could be invited to as a sophomore. I was invited by my junior girlfriends I loved dearly, but a girl who had been bullying me for years was also in the sorority. During initiation week she cornered me at my locker as the bell rang. As a sorority sister she had the authority to tell me to do whatever she wanted, and as an initiate for that week, a.k.a "baby rat," I had to do what any sorority sister told me to do.

She yelled at me to crawl on my knees like a baby to class as the bell rang, when it was obvious I would be late and get in trouble. I was wearing a pacifier around my neck, dressed in pajamas, with a "rat" tail pinned to my rear. Every inch of my pride was already sucked dry in this ridiculous outfit that degraded me and who I was. As she yelled at me to "Do what I say!" I felt tears building in my eyes. I was scared...and then my fear turned to anger. I stood up and yelled, "Hell, no!" I tore off my costume, and as her dark heavily made-up eyes grew wide in disbelief, I threw my costume into the trash and stormed off. She screamed back, "You're kicked out of initiation!" My response was, "I quit!"

Although this experience left me with little faith in sisterhood, I had started to stand in my power. Then, more confusion with relationships—and more substances and food to help ease the pain.

I realize now that the gift inside of all of this pain is that I found my voice and have been able to call in my own love and power. This was Spirit's way of showing me I would never get external validation from anyone and it was up to *me* to love myself unconditionally. Back then, though, I didn't see this and it was one of the most painful times of my life. As alone as I felt, sugar became my comfort. I might not be able to get other people to love or even accept me, but I could soothe myself with food. Being bullied protected me from the pain of not loving myself; I could point my finger at the bullies for making me feel unloved and unworthy. It was their fault!

At fifteen, after rounds and rounds of antibiotics from strep throat or bronchitis, I was tested for allergies. I was allergic to practically everything! I swelled up like a tick by the time I walked out of the doctor's office. We moved forward with allergy shots, and I continued to eat whatever I wanted—not connecting my eating habits and negative thoughts to my miserable existence in my body temple. I still couldn't hear the whispers of my heart. There was too much junk in my system to allow me to connect to my body as the portal into my power.

In college, I started backpacking and hiking, grounding and connecting into the earth. I was depressed and had chronic acne that shattered my confidence every time I looked in a mirror, and I would go into nature to find peace. Peace would come and go, but the anxiety would inevitably return. I used sugar, alcohol, and recreational drugs to numb the anxiety, shame, and disappointments in my life. A victim of my own circumstances, I felt punished. I gave away my power to others to be accepted, and I gave my power away to food so I could feel loved and worthy.

After graduation, I fell in love with rock climbing and kayaking. Connecting with the earth through rock climbing and kayaking brought me into my body. But my cravings for love and acceptance ran deep and I remained in an unhealthy altered state in my body. I experienced a false sense of happiness because adrenaline started to give me the "hit" I craved. It was a full-on addiction! Adrenaline and adventure was the way to my heart and became a false sense of happiness.

In my late twenties, I was working for a non-profit making a difference in the lives of youth through adventure-based programs, and I was in love! But I also suffered from chronic fatigue, hormonal issues, acne, anxiety, and depression. I started to find my power more and more by feeling accomplished at rock climbing and doing things that scared me...often. My body was becoming my portal to connection with myself. Climbing was a moving meditation, and I quickly became addicted to the way it made me feel on every level.

I started to eat healthier, enjoying a smoothie every day. This changed everything. It started to crowd out my cravings for sugars and began to crave salads. I was transforming and finding peace, and people wanted to know what I was doing. So I worked with them to help them take charge of their health, too. I was more clear in my thinking, more connected to my heart, and more authentic with myself and others. I was standing in my power more and more, though still not fully anchored in who I was.

As I was traveling cross country with my then partner, we stopped at a fast food joint for a sweet tea to take my turn at the wheel. We would drive through the night and be in Colorado by the next day. I was exhausted from rock climbing, traveling, and sleeping in our Chevy 78 conversion van. After several minutes of sipping on the sugar-filled toxic concoction, I started sweating profusely and my whole body ached. Within half an hour, I was in tears, trembling, and I knew my body was shutting down. The energy behind that sugar was like pouring gasoline on a forest fire that had been quietly burning. Now I was burning internally, and it was spreading like a wildfire—

my temperature was going up and up and up! By the time we pulled into a Walmart to get a thermometer I was convinced something was really wrong. I was crying and desperate for comfort.

I had a fever of 104 in the middle of Tennessee in our home on wheels. We drove to an urgent care facility and were told that I had a kidney infection that would require antibiotics. This crushed me as I had been making so much progress with my health and clean eating, reducing alcohol and the "bad" sugar. Antibiotics were conventional medicine's response, and I was in a dangerous situation so I took them, vowing to my body that I would start to unravel why my immune system was compromised, why the forest fire, and how to take better care of my vessel.

And then I vowed to share my knowledge with others if I could heal myself first.

I took a deep dive into health, nutrition, hormones, and how to alleviate all my symptoms—and realized sugar was the big perpetrator. I began a meditation and spiritual practice to gain insight on the "why me" mindset and my feelings of victimization.

I realized that this body was my own animal to reckon with and to come to understand. I needed to accept that I had done damage and figure out the best way to clean it up. I was still having symptoms that would cause me to shrivel up and cry each day, but these episodes happened less and less often. Even so, I would start to feel I was making progress and then a new symptom would show up. Doctors and specialists wanted to put me on Lexapro for my anxiety, birth control for my hormones (depression, spotting, acne), and Accutane to take care of the acne once and for all. *No.* My intuition just said, *No, there is something deeper here.* I knew my body had the ability to heal itself. What had gone wrong?

When the anger, fear, or anxiety popped up, I started to sense a different vibration in my body. As I journaled about my highs and lows, I knew that there was a vibrational frequency that would come with both—and I wanted more of the highs. This became my new "hit" and I wanted more of that please. Less sugar, more *real authentic joy,* please.

At thirty-five, I refused medications and let go of my toxic marriage... and my anxiety began to dissipate. I charged forward with all my might into a high-paced real estate career seeking recognition, success, and of course, money! *That should do it!,* I thought. *Once the money comes and I am successful, the acne will die, my confidence will soar, and I will finally be happy and healthy!*

Instead, money pushed me right off my wagon of healthy eating and healthy living. I became a workaholic and poured all my efforts into making others happy...again seeking validation from others, in the forms of receiving checks and, often, thank you gifts. Finally I was good at something. I was successful.

And then BAM...my father got pancreatic cancer and died. I was angry. He was my mentor, best friend, and *biggest* fan. Now what? Who would value me and love me as much as he did? I dove back into nutrition and how to beat cancer and tried to save him, but...I couldn't. I felt like a failure and hated myself. I hated money. I told myself I didn't need any of it. I just wanted to be loved. I had forgotten about the body being my portal into my power. I gave away my power again—to all my clients, my broker—and my happiness was dependent on sales, growth, and working my ass off. Money and success had finally given me what I thought was security. Yet, I was more alone than ever.

I found myself back in yoga classes, weeping through savasana in my sadness and grief. And the poor eating habits had returned along with my stress as well as the acne, depression, anxiety, and, now, weight gain.

And then I heard, "Where is your voice, Dear one?"

I could hear my body whispering gently, "Why have you left me and abandoned me?"

Yoga, as another portal into my body, saved my life this time. I started teaching yoga and movement and was able to move through years of grief. I began to honor my temple with food, exercise, and meditation. My vibration was raising. Things were becoming easier, and I had more ease and grace in my life. The shift was happening, and it was real. I began to plan a move back out West, and then my mother was diagnosed with lung cancer, just five years after my father passed. Devastation landed.

I rented a place near my mother to spend as much time as possible with her, even though it was so painful. I just wanted to save her, to fix her, so she could stay with me forever—but I had no control over it. She was my best friend. It was the hardest lesson in letting go I have ever been through. Sometimes my inner bully still shows up to tell me I didn't do enough. I didn't hold her hand for her last breath. But I couldn't. I had so many wonderful memories with her that I couldn't bear seeing her in pain and medicated and have that be our last memory.

I have learned to accept the way I dealt with my mother's death, and I am gentle on the little girl who did the best she could. Now when the bully shows up, instead of using sugar or alcohol to comfort myself, I connect with my little girl—the one who feels like she didn't do enough—and I tell her it's okay. "You did the best you could, sweetie, in the moment. With all the tools you had, you did the best you could."

And that is what started this divine relationship with myself, nurturing the tiger within, and that's when the feeding frenzy started. The more I nurtured the little girl, loved her, talked to her, and flirted with her in the mirror, the more beautiful I became, inside and out. The more love I had for others, the more compassion I had for myself, the more compassion with which I was able to meet my clients. She empowered me to meet people where they are without judgment and simply love them.

I finally began to see my time as sacred rather than just letting it be filled up. Being busy was just another form of seeking external validation. Now, I was truly enjoying spending time with myself.

My coaching programs grew from focusing on food to focusing on nurturing relationships, self-care, community, and spirituality. I witness my clients shift—when they start to take out the junk that no longer serves them, their divine connection slowly begins to unfold. They feel more aligned, more loved, and more supported.

It's important to realize that we are our best healers and that we intuitively know what is best for ourselves on every level. The key is to remove the habits and foods that are causing inflammation in the body that are also interfering with our connection to our divine source. When we can clear this channel, we will experience support, worthiness, and unconditional love for ourselves—no matter what life throws our way! This empowers us to live fully and choose love.

The feeding and care of our body temple is of utmost importance as it allows us to play, sleep, and be in service doing what we love. The feeding of our divine feminine is what will reach far past our vessel—it will heal the world. When we tap into loving ourselves unconditionally, we give others permission to do the same. And that's how we change the world.

Just be you, and love the hell out of you.

Shannon Lee Nickerson is a mountain lover, wellness advocate, and soul-driven health coach. She specializes in helping women learn how to identify which foods are fueling their bodies and which foods are causing inflammation, stress, and possibly disease. She provides women with tools to find their inner power so they can understand what food and habits fuel their unique bodies, how to  thrive under stress, and how to make healthy habits last without feeling deprived. Her clients consistently share how they lose weight, understand their unique bodies, and have more energy for their life and loved ones.

Shannon Lee has been in the wellness industry for more than seventeen years. She studied at the Institute of Integrative Nutrition, is a board-certified Stress Management Technician, certified yoga teacher, and group fitness instructor. She offers one-on-one private coaching, a 21-Day Group Signature Detox program, and corporate wellness coaching. In corporate wellness coaching, she is known as the Energy Break Queen and offers short customized routines at summits, trainings, leadership events, and conventions. She helps participants move their energy, better assimilate the content, improve clarity and focus, promote camaraderie, and enhance the participants' experience.

In addition to Energy Breaks, Shannon Lee and her team offer on-site fitness classes and corporate wellness programs for employees. The program mission is to reduce healthcare costs by addressing obesity, diabetes, high cholesterol, heart conditions, and stress related illnesses through education in fitness, food, and lifestyle modifications. Participants have experienced reduced sick days, reduced stress, increased productivity, improved sleep, and more fulfillment in their daily lives.

Shannon Lee's mission is to empower men and women to nourish their body, retrain their mind, and connect with their spirit so they can feel good in their body again. The resources, guidance, and tools provided by Shannon Lee have helped hundreds of people take control of their health, rise up, and soar in all areas of their life to live life to the fullest. Learn more at **www.shannonnickerson.com.**

Special Gift

-FREE ebook-

Smoothies To Ditch Cravings For Good

Ditch sugar and beat your cravings for good!
Download at **www.mysmoothiebook.com**

Exploding into Wholeness

BY NADIA MUNLA

I was born during the civil war in Lebanon.

When I was just two years old, a bomb exploded nearby, and the entire windowpane over my crib fell on me. When my father recounts the story, he always boasts that I was a "courageous little baby" because I just lay there quietly under the sheet of glass waiting to be rescued. I did not cry. I did not move. I just lay there.

In my early childhood years, I fell asleep in one room and woke up in the middle of the night being wheeled into another. We spent weeks up in our attic sleeping on mattress pads beside human-sized jars of pickled olives while we played the only board game we had, Monopoly. In our fantasy world, we made big bucks and bought hotels, while in our real life, we were drinking powdered milk and getting one hour of electricity a day.

Although my father attributed my silence under that sheet of glass to courage, I'm pretty sure it was, in fact, shock—and what the trauma world calls "freeze" mode. This incident would become the first of many experiences that instilled in me a deep lack of safety and a slow process of disconnection from my body.

According to many ancient meditation practices, our bodies have seven main chakras, which are wheels of energy in our subtle body from the base of our spine to the crown of our head. Each point has a particular color, vibration, and function, and if everything is working great, we are all technically emanating an array of rainbow colors. The problem is many of us are walking around with our lights dimmed.

Our first (root) chakra is all about safety and grounding. And this was the first color that went dull in my body, at the root of my spine. This was when I learned to hold my breath between every explosion, where I clenched tightly to survival and established that it was me against the world.

Despite some rough circumstances, I had a colorful childhood filled with love, laughs, and lots of not-so-great dance shows I put my family through. From an early age, it became clear that I had an immense passion for dance. I trained every day and had plans to go professional. So much so that when we moved to the United States for a few years, I trained at the Maryland Youth Ballet with my eye on the prize: going on pointe in a tutu.

But those ambitions quickly dissolved when my dance teacher announced that they would not be accepting me into the company because of irregularities in my knees, and I would never be able to successfully dance on pointe without severe pain. I was nine years old, and I had just experienced my first total and utter heartbreak. This is where the next point in my body went quiet. My heart chakra shut down.

After a few attempts at other dance genres, I gave up dance completely. The heartbreak was too much and I chose to shut off my body's natural inclination to emote and express. My body had become an obstacle to my dreams.

The lack of safety and security in my early years was compounded by the discovery of my sexuality in my early teens. It felt like overnight I had become a magnet for unwanted sexual attention—from men on the street, boys at school and, most heartbreakingly, a close relative who was a key father figure in my life.

I had what men wanted and I quickly learned that if I didn't give it away, I was punished. And if I did, I was equally punished. It was here that I learned that my erotic, feminine body was not safe. And so I disconnected from a healthy sensuality and began protecting myself by either completely flatlining or hyper-accentuating. On the map of my body, another light went out. That of my second chakra: the center of pleasure, desire, and creation.

The perfect recipe for disembodiment continued. Polycystic Ovarian Syndrome (PCOS) and debilitating period pain at age twelve, shameful back acne at age fourteen, and bleeding stomach ulcers at age sixteen. I'm still not sure which came first—the hating myself or the literal gut-wrenching pain in my stomach—but either way, there was a constant knot in my solar plexus.

I think it was safe to say that my body and I were not getting along at all. And I definitely did not think there was anything sacred or wise about her. On the contrary. She was the cause of most of my pain and shame.

I spent the next fifteen years doing everything to manage her, silence her, and completely bypass her. Slowly but surely my young vibrant, open, and free body became closed, contracted, and somber. It was as though life had had its way with me—slowly working its way up my body one energy point at a time. The first chakra: safety. The second chakra: sexuality. The third chakra: identity. The fourth chakra: the heart. Everything from my neck down was inaccessible.

What followed was a whole decade of trying to win at life operating from the neck up.

In my late twenties, part of my vision of success involved getting accepted to the University of Southern California's (USC) Peter Stark Program, a prestigious MFA film producing program that accepted only twenty-five students from around the world each year.

I worked at Universal Studios during the day, attended USC from 6 to 11 p.m., and completed classwork after grabbing the only "healthy" option at midnight, an iceberg lettuce salad from the Wendy's drive-through. It was understood that we were choosing to participate in a form of Hollywood hazing, a simulated "survival of the fittest." I slept with my Blackberry under my pillow and woke up at 6 a.m. to read and write coverage on scripts. My body had no place in this brutal schedule, and exercise was what I did when I walked to and from my car.

As a woman, I had the extra burden of proving that I was more than just a sex object or an emotional wreck who couldn't handle the pressure. I can't even recount the number of times I had to stay silent about the sexual advances by powerful men or, even worse, the emotional abuse when the sexual advances were refused. During that time, even my wardrobe reflected an asexual nature to it. Black tanks and khakis on set, blazer and jeans on the lot. Whatever I could do to blend in and avoid unwanted attention.

It was at this point in my life, exhausted and disconnected, that I found freedom in the last place I would have ever imagined: a pole-dancing studio. When I walked in my first day, my body exhaled for the first time in years.

As I moved on my mat in the soft glow of red lighting, I felt like I was back in the womb. I remember our teacher guiding us to slow down, breathe, and sink into our curves. I remember delighting in the feeling of my hair tickling my cheek while I stretched into a luxurious long swirl. I remember feeling excitement at a secret I had found deep in my being. Like a cat, I found myself purring my way to pleasure and never wanting to leave again.

And so began the journey back home to my body. Right away, I signed up for weekly classes. Saturdays at 4 p.m. became my church. And before I knew it, I had signed up to get certified as an instructor.

During those years, I moved from Los Angeles to New York to produce and co-direct my first feature film under my production company, and on my thirtieth birthday, I happily gathered a huge group of friends to celebrate two huge milestones: the distribution of my film and getting certified as a feminine movement teacher.

Looking back, it's so glaringly obvious that each of these milestones represented the two different paths I was being presented, a life where I continued to live from the neck up and a life where I could reclaim my embodied essence through fierce femininity, sacred sexuality, and an honoring of my body's innate wisdom.

Until then, I had somehow managed to push through the sleepless nights and $3 on-set burritos, fueled by a deep fear of losing at the game. It took another full year of suffering at a New York ad agency before my body finally hit a breaking point. She had gotten a taste of pleasure and was *not* accepting anything less than that.

In one fell swoop, I quit my day job, closed my production company, and leapt straight into the unknown world of coaching.

My body began to light up again. Instead of continuing to succumb to the stories of how my body should look like, feel like, or be managed, I asked how can I repair our relationship by listening, loving, and learning from her? How can I understand her yes's and her no's and truly honor them? How can I nourish her with pleasure instead of manage her with deprivation? How can I love her with confidence and trust instead of fighting her with my "shoulds"?

As I healed my relationship with my body, and as she took center stage in my decisions, I began to lean into a world where winning at life actually looked like embodying my ecstasy through a cultivation of safety, through an honoring of my internal seasons, and through an awakening of my inner Aphrodite.

I began to guide women through this process in my movement classes and coaching practice with the portal being sensuality, pleasure, and permission.

This bliss trickled into my own life. I had cultivated a beautiful life partnership with a man who helped me soften and flow even more. The relationship opened my eyes to a reality I'd never experienced—a life with adventure, freedom, and so much pleasure. The more I became embodied, the more I felt connected to my essence, to the world around me, and ultimately to God/dess.

Cut to three and a half years later. I'm in the Sacred Valley, Peru. It's nighttime.

The smells of tobacco, palo santo, and vomit waft through the air of the temple I'm in.

I'm lying under layers of thick alpaca blankets while I stare at the stars wondering why on earth I chose *this* over margaritas on the beach with my man. I'm pulled out of my self-flagellation by the sound of vomiting coming from my neighbor who I'm convinced is going to die in ceremony.

In addition, my soul has perfectly timed my ceremony to the *one* holiday a year when Peruvians celebrate with fireworks. With every pop, my body contracts. I keep getting smaller and smaller, tighter and tighter, shrinking so much I'm hoping I might just disappear.

The plant medicine we drank that night was ayahuasca, known as the "rope of death" because she basically shows you the darkest dragons of your psyche and asks you to slay them. As I lay in the dark for hours in our ceremonial cave, I understand the true meaning of terror.

I did not fully understand this as it was happening but I know now that I had turned right back into the two year old little girl who froze under the sheet of glass. And to protect her, came a nihilistic warrior whose swords were drawn and who trusted nothing and no one, because, well, explosions.

She drew her swords and held her breath for the next sound, which in my case, kept exploding all night. My inner warrior didn't trust the Shaman. She didn't trust the plants. She didn't trust the process. She trusted nothing except her ability to fight. Five hours felt like a lifetime.

I thought I would return from Peru with a deeper connection to God/dess, and instead I found myself more confused and angry. And it just got worse. Soon after I got back, my partner ended our relationship without an explanation. Suddenly, every version of home disappeared: my partner's loving arms, my Brooklyn apartment, and my life in New York City. In addition, my complicated immigration status meant I was facing the possibility of getting deported if I couldn't sort out my papers. Sprinkle in a failed launch and an IRS audit and my swords were drawn and *ready* for battle.

You would think this would be my rock bottom. But it wasn't. Chaos is my comfort zone, and I battle pretty damn well when everything feels unsafe. What I don't do well when things are unsafe is have faith.

But I hadn't realized that yet. Which is why my rock bottom actually came nine months later.

I was sitting on my bed winding down from a Fourth of July picnic when I heard *pop pop pop*. From one second to another I went right back to the ceremony in Peru. I tried to nurture myself through it, but this time my body hit a new breaking point and I completely fell apart.

For about three weeks, I had a mystery illness. No one could figure out what was wrong with me.

I was utterly confused. I knew my physical body so well. Why were none of my usual healing go-tos working?

I felt betrayed. I felt hopeless. I found myself back at the point in my life where I had no idea how to interpret what my body was telling me. Again, I felt like it was me against the world. I had no idea what to do. I just felt like I was being sucked back into the same old struggle I had as a teenager with my PCOS and ulcers.

My intuition kept telling me that I was being asked to deepen my relationship to my body in a way I hadn't so far. By this point, I had basically mastered nourishing my physical, hormonal, and emotional body. But what I hadn't yet fully understood was my energetic body.

I had gone for all types of healing, and each time, I would feel like I was completely fine for twenty-four hours and then would relapse into worse pain. I needed this suffering to end once and for all.

Luckily, I was working with an energy coach at the time, so on our next session, I told her I was exhausted and couldn't take it anymore. The illness had all started with a bizarre spasm in my throat and so together, we journeyed into my throat to see what was going on. With her guidance, I was horrified to discover that I had remnants of energetic debris from the war explosions lodged in different crevices of my throat and lungs.

The moment she pointed it out, I began to cough and cough and cough. And it did not stop. For days I laid on the floor of my room, trusting that my body was releasing years and years of dark energy that wasn't mine. I lost my voice. My bones felt like they were breaking. And my diaphragm went into full spasm, which is *fantastic* when you have a cough.

Now let me tell you, there was definitely a part of me that thought this was all insane. Was I really going to tell my assistant to reschedule my coaching calls because I was coughing up the remnants of dead people?

But I had no choice but to cancel life and stare at my ceiling wondering, why?

On one of those days, as my phone played a rendition of "Ra Ma Da Sa" for the 777th time, it hit me. My relationship to God/dess had always been through pleasure, but when it came to pain, I shut down into complete nihilism. And I would oscillate between complete resignation and warrior mode. Me against the world. Me waiting for the next explosion. And my nervous system just didn't want to do it anymore.

My body that had clenched for years, waiting in apprehension for the next explosion was ready to heal. She was ready to finally let go. And the only way she was going to heal was if my nihilistic warrior stopped trying to fight everything.

I had to lay down her swords—not through resignation, but rather through surrender. It was time to make peace with God.

Something took over me, and I grabbed my purple Post-it pad to write something, and out flowed: "I trust you. I have faith in you. Through light and dark. Always and forever, I love you."

I looked at the words, swirling them around in my mouth. Feeling their truth. I tore off the paper and began to fold it slowly and intentionally. As I did this, I realized what I had jotted down with a ballpoint pen on a wrinkled Post-it were actually my vows to God. And since I don't believe in an old man in the sky but rather a universal energy, I realized it was also a vow to myself.

I looked at my altar. On it lay an empty heart locket that had previously contained an anniversary love note from my ex. I had just burnt it on the last full moon. And today, by divine timing, was the new moon.

I was ready. Ready to welcome in a love affair with faith, a co-creation with God, and a lifelong union with my body, through dark and light. I took the folded Post-It note, placed it in the locket, and put it around my neck.

"I trust you. I have faith in you. Through light and dark. Always and forever, I love you.

That's when it dawned on me that I had basically just married myself.

And there I was.

It wasn't the wedding I had dreamed of as a kid. It wasn't me at Burning Man with my friends witnessing my statement of self-love. It was just me on the floor with unwashed hair, in my pajamas and a pile of tissues—and God/dess. It was just me, fully present, sitting in the sacred wisdom of my body. And it was enough.

Nadia Munla is an Embodiment Coach who guides womxn to sensual nourishment and embodied power by helping them reconnect to their own bodies. She is immensely passionate about supporting womxn in their journey back to their embodied essence so they can feel vibrant, alive, feminine, and free again.

Through her one-on-one coaching, Embody dance classes, and Embody teacher training Nadia has guided thousands of womxn across five continents on their journey back to themselves. You can find her at **www.nadiamunla. com, embodydanceclass.com** or join the conversation at The Embody Tribe FB group.

From Contained Mess to Embodied Flow

BY DENA OTRIN

My journey of self-love, being kind to my body, and honoring all the goodness within me began many years ago when an amazing woman walked into my life one day in a networking meeting talking about Reiki. Reiki is a form of energy healing used to help move blocked or pent-up energy within the body and mind. Intuitively I felt drawn to her and the practice of Reiki, and I still remember that moment of saying to myself that I thought she could help me.

This was the first time I was even open to the possibility of working on my past wounds that I had carried in my body for decades. My body would not let me forget; it would still react and keep me stuck as a prisoner in a cell of past memories and painful experiences.

But finally, I was able to release the flooding of emotions and of events that had consistently shown up over the years. I was finally ready to look in the mirror and see myself without being bombarded by negative thoughts. I could stop tearing myself apart—one body part at a time—since I had gained weight and had turned to food for "emotional healing." I was ready let go of what was not mine in the first place and release myself of shame, blame, and guilt. All these thoughts were tantalizing but scary as hell. When you have not faced your wounds, the thought of going near them can be petrifying. I had come to expect and depend on feeling uneasy and putting myself down. Despite how much I hated it, it was a constant, a known expectation and something I had put so much energy into pushing down and hoping it would just go away. Hoping I would start loving myself as others in my life loved me. My mind and body would not forget and kept bringing up what I need to heal. So for the first time I felt like I could begin my healing process.

The crazy twist for me was that I am a trained professional counselor and was always an empath and present, available, and comforting to everyone but myself. I felt like traditional therapy was not the path for me, because I did not want to just talk about what was already so painful to acknowledge. I needed something else, and Reiki immediately caught my interest as something different. It was a technique where I did not have to "relive" experiences by talking about them and feeling triggered even more. It is a technique focusing on healing energy that comes only from a place of love... and I needed a lot of self-love right now. To me, that in itself was nonthreatening, and instead of being a crying mess on a couch I could be relaxed and comforted on a massage table. That is what I needed. That is where I was.

So I made my first appointment with excitement, hesitation, and hope. I remember needing to breathe deeply in the car as I made my way to the appointment. I gave myself affirmations of encouragement and praise for finally taking this step. The first is the hardest. My stomach was tight, my head hazy, but I was not going to give up on myself again...not this time. Not as I had done so many other times in my life with many things. I was worth healing. I deserved to feel better.

Here I was entering the threshold of the office and the hopes of a new beginning in my life. We started with some discussion of what brought me to the appointment, which I remember thinking, "I was hoping I did not have to do this, I just want to be on the table." The discussion was not as painful as I had imagined, though. I cried a little, but was not consumed with tears as I expected to be. I think I was still protecting myself, keeping up my walls and afraid to let myself fully feel. Telling my whole story of hurt and negativity toward myself could lead to judgment—my biggest fear since I spent enough time judging myself. My body could not take someone else judging me. There was no room. I had filled it up to the point that it had spilled over into depression. I was full to capacity and now my only option was to begin releasing it. I had exploded in anger too many times, been critical of loved ones too many times, and I was tired of the need to control everyone in my life for fear of being hurt. I was a contained mess.

On the outside, I was a pulled together professional with control of my life.

On the inside, my mess was a dark ominous cloud growing up my body and affecting me more than I wanted to admit or even realized. I thought I could control my own emotions, not think about it and hoped it would just go away. But of course it did not ever go away, as nothing does when it needs attention. It keeps rearing its ugly head and wreaking havoc on my body, mind, and soul.

So here I was taking the biggest step to finally help myself. As I spoke, I felt no judgment. This did surprise me, how much my negative self-talk had skewed my view of myself and what others may think of me being a professional counselor that had not healed herself. Instead of being questioned, judged, or made to feel guilty for my thoughts and behaviors, I was presented with the powerful truth that I am a loved individual who deserves to feel as if the sky just opened up and showered me with all the stars in the galaxy. I am someone who deserves happiness and self-kindness and no longer has to live within the walls I have created and memories I have kept. Great thoughts, but how was I to get there?

I can tell you that my healing process began on the massage table that day. I was lying on the table surrounded by beautiful crystals and relaxing music, a powerful woman at the head of the table who has the gift of Reiki and Spiritual Guidance with her every step of the way. She placed her hands along the top and sides of my head and tapped into my energy very quickly. As she began her work, I laid with my eyes closed and a single tear started to stream out of my eye. Then an amazing event occurred where I could feel movement in my belly, which later I discovered was my Sacral Chakra and where the Inner Child resides. With this movement I started to feel a tug from my belly going up my chest, over my face, and out through my head. When the energy got to my face I was seeing flashbacks of moments in time from my childhood and early teen years, some of which I had forgotten. It flew past my eyes so fast like a split-second movie montage of scenes in my life. I could sense my eyes were looking in all directions as the images swiftly passed right by me and out through the crown of my head. It was intense, but it was amazing to see and feel this happening. I was actually getting past wounds pulled out from my belly so I no longer could hold onto them anymore. This is exactly what I needed!

In our second session, as I lay on the massage table she placed me into a guided meditation connecting me with people that I needed to talk to in helping my healing process even more and begin the practice of forgiveness. In this guided meditation I received knowledge I needed to begin forgiving others for wounds I had held onto for way too long. I felt comforted and at peace with those I connected with and was able to feel forgiveness toward them. It was an emotional and life-changing meditation. After this session I went home and cried from this release of energy and looked into the mirror, as I was encouraged to do as the session ended. This time as I looked in the mirror I saw the most beautiful blue eyes I had ever seen. I was told to look into the mirror at my eyes because now I could now see my true soul within my eyes. It was amazing that I could see beauty and love for myself in my reflection that I had not felt in years. This began another layer of transformation and the emergence of my true self, the love and light I possessed and the power and wisdom my body had to keep telling me to seek help and heal. My spirit and soul knew I was deserving of this healing. Now I was finally mentally ready to accept it and give kindness and love to myself... body, mind, and spirit.

I had a few more sessions, and as time went on I started to see energetic shifts happening with others I had forgiven. I noticed our interactions were more pleasant, positive, and no longer emotionally charged with negativity. I also began to see the love and beauty within myself and began allowing myself to have fun, to honor my needs a little more, and to voice my own thoughts and feelings in more healthy ways as opposed to not voicing them at all or being curt and controlling to those around me. It was a pleasant change. I started to feel happier inside my body, and can say I no longer had depressed feelings. I was changing. My thoughts were changing, and my relationships were changing. It was about time.

The next phase of healing I did was within a group focused on healing the Inner Child. It was online and over the phone since group participants were from all over the country. It was run by the same amazing women as the spiritual guide and energy healer for us all. This was an incredible project because I was able to release even more wounds, self-doubt, and feelings of negativity toward myself. I was releasing old patterns of thoughts and scripts from my past and I was taking the needle from the record player off the same old record that ran through my mind and kept my body stuck. Layer by layer, I was letting go of past wounds. Big, small, important or insignificant ones—I was letting them go. My body was happily letting this happen, too. As I became present and aware to my thoughts and feelings and no longer trying to push them down, there was no resistance from my body or mind anymore. Long before I accepted it emotionally, my body knew that I had to work on letting go of what no longer served me any purpose. So that is what I finally began doing.

From this amazing experience I became a member of an energy healing group. This group allowed me to have time to focus on myself by listening to my needs, honoring them, and exploring what they are in a safe and supportive environment. We used mediation, guided imagery, grounding techniques, yoga poses, movement, and music to connect with our higher spiritual selves and continue with our healing process. Having discovered how well energy healing works and how it can be life changing, I soon became certified as a Reiki III practitioner.

After a few years of attending the energy healing groups, I began to tap back into my childhood passion of movement and dance. Every time I have seen a Reiki practitioner—which I now love to attend for spiritual guidance—I am told to get back into dance. My inner child *wants* to dance. I know this! I can feel it strongly at times. It is in my future to get trained in dance movement therapy, which I wanted to do when I was an eighteen-year-old college student, but no program even existed then.

So the next best practice of movement was presented to me on social media, an advertisement for a Yoga Teacher Training program at a local studio near where I live. I saw the ad and thought that would be interesting, but I had gone to a yoga class once before and that was all the experience I had. So I let my mind take over to tell me why that would be silly of me to do with no experience, but the information kept presenting itself to me and I decided to listen to my body instead of my head and learned more about the program. What I loved about the program is that I needed to go to yoga every week for myself as part of the training. This was huge since I was not doing much for myself as far as movement of energy within my body. I had heard how great yoga is for your mind, body and soul, but I never gave myself permission to go to a class. So now I had the accountability I needed and would make the effort to go. I had not realized how much you learn about yourself and let go of on the mat. Yoga allows me to challenge myself with asanas at my own pace and within my own practice. I am also able to let go of my inner critic and tap into my power on the mat. I set an intention or say a mantra each time I step onto my mat. I can move, breathe, and release what I need to let go of in one session. It truly is a practice for my mind, body, and soul, and it has been a gift to complete my 200-hour certification as a yoga teacher.

I am excited and proud of my journey right now. I'm living my purpose as a therapist and have also created an online business called An Empowered

Life—which is what I've created for myself and what I help others do, too. Listening to my body and letting go of what no longer serves my higher self is a continuous effort since I am always faced with new challenges—because, after all, that's just what life is. However, the key is to not let those challenges become wounds that only foster more self-doubt and self-judgment. I have learned to handle my life in wonderful new ways that benefit everything, especially my relationships. I now listen to the wisdom of my body and my intuition, and use my yoga practice to let go of stress and doubt. I am finally honoring all of me!

Dena Otrin has been in the health and wellness field for 20 years as a Licensed Professional Coun- selor and in private practice for 18 years, currently at Bayside Coun- seling in Connecticut. Dena is a certified Reiki III practitioner, a Life Transformation practitioner, health and wellness consultant, facilitator of women's retreats, workshops and empowerment Groups, and a self-empowerment  blogger through her business An Empowered Life. Adding to her reper- toire of holistic services for health, wellness, self-care, and self-love, Dena recently became a Certified Yoga Teacher and a Certified Yoga Teacher for Kids. Dena embodies empowerment as she assists others on their journey of personal or business transformation and success. Learn more at **www.AnEmpoweredLife.net**.

Hips Don't·Lie

BY BERNADETTE PLEASANT

Most people believe you need to have rhythm to dance—that all you need is rhythm and courage and you can just get up and do it. Or they believe you need to have a "don't care" mentality in order to dance. I'd like to offer that sometimes there are other reasons why people don't dance.

It's early March and Ron has come upstairs with coffee in hand. He makes the most *amazing* cup of coffee and says it's his way of saying, "I love you" every day. I sit in bed inhaling the scents of today's brew; it's my favorite, cafe mocha with a healthy dose of cinnamon. It's too hot, so I wait. My laptop is perched on my lap and I am about to jump into the day's planning. The Martha Stewart show is playing in the background. I'm not that into her, but I overhear something that sounds very un-Martha Stewart like.

I glance up and see a pole...as in *stripper pole*. I do a double take and immediately think of a song that I heard on Sesame Street as a child: *One of these things just doesn't belong here.* Martha Stewart is sharing the screen with this beautiful brunette who begins to move in such a way that you can hear music. It's like watching music move through her body. She's very different than Martha Stewart, who seems to have no music in her body. The brunette deepens into her hips, deliciously pulling on her clothes, while her hands move on her body exploring it unapologetically—not in an overtly sexual way, but in a way that is unmistakable...she is enjoying her own curves. Her wrists delicately explore the hills and valleys of her sacred body. She moves in a way that is an extension of her breath. It is so natural and delicious and I am captivated. She does a brief routine and introduces her company. She speaks of pole dancing and my only point of reference is the time I found myself in a strip club—but the demonstration she's doing looks and feels very different. She looks like she gains more pleasure than any spectator could, which only magnetizes me more to the beauty I see.

I feel a longing in my body to fall deeply in love with myself like her. And I know that she can help me find out how. I take another sip of my delicious cup of coffee and hear myself say to Ron, "You know, my birthday is in a couple months and I heard the woman on the screen mention that she has a school in New York. They offer birthday parties. Maybe I should go pole dancing for my birthday..." Ron looks surprised. Then I say, "Maybe I should take a group of my friends pole dancing for my birthday." Again, Ron looks at me surprised and asks, "Do you think that your friends would be interested in this?"

One more sip of this coffee and I'm ready to face the day. I pick my phone up, feeling courageous, and send out a group text to ten or so friends: "Hey ladies, I'm thinking about taking a pole dancing class for my birthday. Who's game?" Moments later the beeps are coming in like Fourth of July fireworks. One woman after another tells me how she has secretly wanted to do this and she's in. Another says her leg is in a cast, but she'd sure like to come and watch. Before I knew it, a party was being formed.

I eagerly schedule the class during the week of my birthday and we are given the simple instruction: Don't wear lotion. *What the fuck?! We are black women. We go nowhere with dry skin.* I reach out to each of my friends to remind them of the "no lotion" rule, and convince each woman that she will be okay in the dark cover of night.

We arrived at the studio and it was nothing like I had expected. There we each stood feeling uncomfortable in shorts and tank tops. Lisa wore leggings because she refused to show her skin, and I know Roslyn was wearing lotion. There were no mirrors. The room was dimly lit with lots of candles. It was sexy! Moments later, in walked this very small-framed white woman and as she stood there among us I started to notice my friends speaking in code. It's just a look, like a silent language we black women speak. We were silently asking, "What does this little white woman have for us?" After all, dancing is in our blood.

After a brief introduction she started the music. I watched this woman start to speak a language of love with her body that I did not recognize. She took her time as she slowly melted into movement. How did she move so slowly? How did her body continue to ripple and stretch into curves more deeply than I thought possible? She took a deep breath and offered directions. We couldn't take our eyes off of her.

I swear this woman would take those hips around the room wiping every single wall with them. The way she moved was slow, intentional, and sensual. I loved to dance, and I knew I was physically capable of moving my hips in that way. Yet, there was something about this kind of movement that was different. It was not at all mindless, which is how I normally danced. When moving to syncopated beats, my movement was short and mimicked the staccato sounds of the music. When slow dancing, I was usually partnered and focused my attention on the other person and not my own experience.

In this classroom, the movement was meditative. The focus was internal and the teacher encouraged us to engage with every sensual thing. But when I went to send my hips out, something happened. I could not bring myself to fully extend and unlock my hips. I couldn't push my booty back and rotate my pelvis enough to create the wide and sexy circles that I loved watching the instructor create. This movement brought an awareness to each particular region of the body I had become disconnected from. Even with practice, it just wasn't happening. Something shut me down.

I later discovered, after much soul-searching, that this was not a physical limitation. This movement brought focus and memories were flooding back. This was an emotional block. This move and the "audacity" of it, brought me back emotionally to a childhood trauma that literally was stuck inside my body. What shut me down was a memory of my mother's eyes. You see, my stepfather molested me as a child. When my mom became aware of the abuse, sadly, it sparked disconnect between her and me. And while she didn't say anything to me, her eyes would sometimes say disapprovingly, "That's too much. That's enough."

So here I am a grown woman standing in this classroom and my hips are on lockdown. It wasn't a physical lockdown—this was very much emotional. Emotionally, in this class, I could see my mother's eyes saying, "That's too much. That's enough. Nice girls don't do that. You may bring on some unwanted situation." And so I was unable to move my hips.

What comes to mind is we were asked to do hip circles, a seemingly easy movement. The instructor invited us to push our ass back to the wall behind us and use our entire glorious ass to paint that wall. Her words that were full and unapologetic—and intentionally feminine. There was no apology whatsoever to be found with the idea of smearing our asses in our minds eye all over the wall behind us. There was a freedom in it. She then asked that we drag our hips around to the left and that we begin to fill the space to the left. I wanted to smear my entire black ass around these walls! She invited us to pull on our clothes and to put our hands slowly on our bodies and to breathe. The hypnotic, slow music matched. She encouraged us to move slower than we ever moved before. To take our time. To move at a pace that only worked for our individual bodies. The music that played was slow and thick and seemed to lick at the walls like our curves were being encouraged to do. This music penetrated every cell. It wrapped around my bones. It gave me permission to move in a way that I had never moved before. *Slow.* I truly wanted to melt into curves like this instructor was moving. I wanted to move so slowly and comfortably, deepening my hips into every corner as I slowly worked them around. But what I noticed was my reach—my hips were not able to cross, stretch, and reach at their full capacity. It was certainly not due to anything physical. We were encouraged to surrender into the safety of the experience. What I saw behind my closed eyes were the eyes of my mother giving me that look that said, "That's too much. Nice girls don't do that. Christian girls don't do that. After all we were raised Jehovah Witnesses."

I felt shame in my hips. I felt shame and I also felt the internal conflict inside my head. My mother's eyes had won. Here I was celebrating my forty-fifth birthday—a married woman with a grown daughter—and my mother's eyes could still affect the way I moved in the world. I knew for certain that I wanted to move inside the safety of this classroom. When the class came to an end and while we all had a wonderful experience, I felt like I received a hit of some unknown euphoric drug. It was an experience I knew I had to come back to.

I eagerly signed up and could not wait to get back. In the weeks before my class began, I would revisit in my mind's eye what happened in that classroom that evening with my mother's eyes and the shame I felt. What *was* that? Whatever it was, I knew it was time for it to change and to go away. I wanted to have the experience *that* teacher was having. I wanted to move with *that* kind of freedom and lightness.

I realized I had a choice to make and so I began to do the work. First, I had to acknowledge that the limiting philosophy of "being too much" was not my own. It wasn't, in fact, too much to have freedom in my hips, ass, and pelvis. *I didn't need to be afraid of the power that existed there.* Some predator's inability to control their urges was not my problem. I did not need to limit my body and joy to someone else's warped sense of understanding.

I realized that I was desiring this movement that seemed so natural—like it was something I should have been doing all along. *When did I stop dancing?* I was also aware that I would never stop dancing. Not this time. After all, I'm forty-five now and it's time for me to stop living the restricted life that was imposed on me. It was time to do something that I was being inexplicably called to do—time to follow my *own* guidance. There was something in this movement. I wasn't learning a new move, but that I was remembering something ancient, carnal, and raw.

"Doing the work" meant I had to stay present and show up in my discomfort. I could not bypass what was emerging. I was aware of the discomfort—it was like wearing a really tight garment that hinders every breath and constricts every inhalation. I would get seeps of air in where I could, but it was never the full expansion. This feeling of not being able to receive a deep inhale felt like my mother was literally riding my back.

I could have stopped going to class. This class made me aware of something and that "something" made me feel uncomfortable. Despite my discomfort, I was curious about what was coming up for me. I wanted to know *what* it was and *why* it was. I found value in investigating this, rather than recoiling and avoiding. I had to be courageous enough to unearth what was emerging.

"Doing the work" also meant that I could not keep still. I unearthed my freedom from this subconscious emotional block by moving. Our connected tissue stores emotional and physical memories. Studies done on movement and connected tissue show us how these memories and trauma are released. By creating blood flow and intentionally focusing on a specific area of the body using slow movement, we unearth that which is ready to come up and be cleared out.

My entire experience was one of birthing. There was joy and pain. Things emerged that I did not want to remember. I would have rather kept them put away! Luckily, this deep dive, unearthing, and emotional work came at a time in my life when I was conscious, sober, and emotionally equipped to deal with it in a healthy way. I could contend with those memories without feeling victim to them, and it allowed me the grace to understand that the look in my mother's eyes was her way of dealing with her own trauma.

Now I send these hips across the street. I send these hips across our nation. I send them into outer space. I have now created an entire mindful movement practice around this very experience because of the value it provides. Staying in the movement keeps me emotionally open and in-tune. By staying with it and by moving, I no longer have any emotional limitations. Moving my body in this way has allowed me to love the parts of my body that I had become disconnected from. That disconnection was subconscious—I wasn't even aware I was disconnected from my own sensuality. I could be sexual, but sensuality was a very different experience. Now, sensuality means taking the time to taste, touch, feel, breathe, and really relish in all my curves. This movement practice keeps me sensual in a way that no longer allows for disconnection. In the past, I listened and experienced from the head up and the thighs down. I was disconnected from a space in my body that hadn't been mine since my own childhood. There was so much subconscious shame around my body that, prior to the initial class, I didn't have ownership of it. Now for the first time, I could really focus on how pleasurable it was to put attention on my body from this place of utter adoration without shame. The hip circles allowed me to push out the shame that was there. Every roll around, I was able to clear out what didn't belong.

I also soon came to learn that the life experiences specific to my trauma that had to be healed in the mindful movement practice, had bigger effects around the rest of my life. Areas of my life where I felt discomfort outside the classroom began to go through an evolution and heal, too.

I became fearless and asked questions when I noticed resistance towards anything and I'd be more inclined to push forward.

These hips are telling a new story. A story of freedom. And they move because my mind has opened. My mind has healed. My heart and my soul have healed. And so now I dance with freedom and without the emotional shackles.

Experiencing this emotional freedom in my movement has allowed for new possibilities to come into my life. It's given me more space to practice empathy and grace. I'm now able to recognize others who are experiencing a block around expressing themselves, either verbally or with the body. I can empathize because *I've been there*. Through my childhood, I had become an expert in making emotional calculations. You know what I'm talking about, don't you? It's when you survey a room and adjust your emotional expressions based on the energy of others. If you have ever girdled, stifled, or half-assed your joy or your pain because someone that you so wished to share it with could not receive it, you have been emotionally calculating. My healing journey through sensual movement has taught me empathy and an understanding of what people go through in this experience, and I am clear around my mission to create and hold space for others as they express themselves through the body, too.

Somehow, we have all learned to work in a narrow margin of emotional range. This has become the new norm. This is what's acceptable. This is what's okay. This is how we were trained to behave. Yet, have you ever seen a toddler hold back? A toddler will let you know how they feel when they are pissed off. Children will let you know when they are happy. They use their entire body. They use their voice. They use their hands and toes. Everything is included. But something happens at some point along the way, perhaps subtly. Or they are told "shush" too many times. Or perhaps more overtly they are told, "That's too much. Stop." Our shame is built around these emotions, and we learn to girdle them. We learn to stifle them. We learn to contort ourselves emotionally to work within this narrow margin.

In my practice, we create and hold space for others to express the full range of their emotions. We practice what it feels like to move our joy without holding back. We practice what it feels like to move rage, knowing that it will pass. We go on what's called an "emotional tour" so that we don't get stuck in just one emotion.

This work mimics the weather. Some days are gloriously sunny and it's just beautiful and your face is up. Sometimes there is a storm coming, and sometimes it's an earthquake. But none of it lasts forever. Emotions come and go just like the weather, if we would only give ourselves that latitude.

I look forward to a world where we give ourselves permission to *feel* and just *be.* By doing this, we really get to be comfortable with our own emotional range. So when we see someone else experiencing some weather, we can hold space for that. We witness them shedding those tears or screaming out that rage they are feeling. We don't shame them or shush them or tell them that's too much. We let them have their moment because we don't get over things, we get through them. It is my firm belief that there are no good, bad, light or dark emotions, only emotions that need to be fully expressed.

Keep moving those hips.

Intoxicating and energetic, **Bernadette Pleasant** is a fiery sensual Speaker, Somatic Healer, and Creator of Femme! She facilitates transformation for those who desire to live out loud through a physical, emotional, and immersive journey. With certifications in The Nia Technique®, Nia® 5 Stages, Ageless Grace®, Pole Dance, Somatic Healing, Reiki, and Integrated Energy Therapy, as well as studies  in African, Tribal, and Free Dance, Bernadette promotes emotional freedom through movement and storytelling.

As a gifted healer, dancer, and entrepreneur, she channels her personal journeys and her radical empathy into transformative, immersive experiences that empower and celebrate people of all genders, ages, sizes, and fitness levels. She comes from a long line of natural healers who have used touch and movement to help others find peace, empowerment, and wellness. Bernadette travels globally leading discussions and inclusive movement on emotional healing through classes, private workshops, retreats, and conference engagements. Learn more at **www.livefemme.com.**

Special Gift

FREE ebook: "Self Care Tips No Matter How Busy You Are"
Do you know the deliciousness of self-care? You might have glimpsed it for a few minutes, a couple of hours or even a number of days. Those precious moments when you don't have to think about anybody else but you. Time to remind yourself of who you truly are—your needs, your aspirations, your desires. That opportunity to fall in love with yourself and treat yourself with the kindness and respect befitting of your loved ones. That's the power of self-care. It fuels us to perform with greater energy and focus. It empowers us to be more resilient and prepares us to deal with challenges that may come our way. It inspires us to be kinder to others and the world around us. The benefits are as diverse as we are.

So how can we consistently carve out that space for ourselves? How do we make me-time a habit—that is, something that is so ingrained in us that it becomes difficult to avoid or give up? We do so by beginning to create rituals and practicing them as often as we can until they take hold and transform our lives! Not having enough time is often the biggest barrier and so, we're removing it! We've come up with ideas for you to practice self-care, no matter how busy you are! **Get access: www.mailchi.mp/livefemme.com/selfcareritualebook**

In the Attic: Birth, Death, and Rebirth of the Naked Yoga Goddess

BY KIMBERLY D. SIMMS

Imagine the horror of being confident and prepared for your life and in the blink of an eye, a gut punch to your confidence—the solar plexus—unexpectedly knocks you off your path and leaves you naked and afraid. That's how I felt: lost, isolated, and alone, with zero self-confidence. It was probably the lowest point of my life—the ending to everything I thought I was. Little did I know, it wasn't. This is my story of birth, death, and rebirth—how being in a place where I felt the most naked and afraid was also my gateway and entry point to power. I began truly shedding old layers of myself that no longer served me. I realized, that year, that I was the architect of my life.

I've always desired to feel safe, loved, and free at all times and in all ways—that's the naked truth. When I felt safe, loved, and free my family did, too. Asa mother of four, I was tired of bouncing between being a martyr for my family one day by giving my blood, sweat, and tears, and the next day a raging, manipulative, frustrated bitch.

When I first became a mother, I wasn't happy and I lost myself. It felt like someone had locked me in an attic and hid the key. I was the someone with the key but I didn't know it yet. But the opportunity to unlock my freedom came in the form of an email from my Yoga studio owner. She invited me and some other yoga teachers from the studio to Miami. I knew I needed a vacation. I had no idea why I was going to Miami, but I knew I needed to go. The day to day routine of being busy and unfulfilled was making me cranky all the time. I knew that being an angry yoga teacher wasn't me..

I got to the Miami Convention Center and walked into what I thought was a cult revival meeting—300 screaming white women, pink boas, a lot of glitter, and feathers exploded in a dimly lit room. "What in the hell have I stepped into?" was the first thought that came to mind, and the next thought was, "White women are crazy." At the center of it all was the craziest of all white women named Regena Thomashauer or *Mama Gena*. She was a women's empowerment guru who curated tools for women to fulfill all their desires. All I knew, as a woman of color, was that my solutions couldn't possibly be the same as hers. But the more I listened to Mama Gena talk about pleasure, desire, and sisterhood the more I could feel a shift in my awareness.

My imagination wildly inspired the real possibility of my own personal desires being fulfilled. I felt myself changing! Imagine life unfolding one desire at a time, one pleasurable moment after the next until you are overflowing in your life with juicy opportunity. Mama Gena gave me the permission I needed to think outside the "attic." I desired to parent from a place of pleasure. I desired to walk my journey with my children—not in front of or behind them, but side by side. This new affinity for pleasure parenting created a wave of love for me by me. It started with how I viewed myself as a woman in a woman's body. I began to understand fully what it meant to be in my body, because my body felt good. I *felt* glorious and *was* glorious! My husband and I found new passion, and we conceived our fourth baby.

Now that my life was about pleasure, I desired a pleasurable labor and delivery. I had an orgasmic birth—the same body parts that made the baby, are the same parts that birth the baby. I used my little bullet and self pleasured during my contractions. It helped balance the pain with the pleasure. I took on that labor like a pro! I was amazed by my body.

Postpartum, I built my yoga practice back up—and it felt so good. It was in the Yoga studio where I learned to allow my body to be my guide. To explain if I should sleep more, eat better, or even open my heart and love harder. After this birth, I felt more gratitude for everything...my family, friends, being a Yogi, and especially for my body. I was attuned with the unique way I could communicate with my body on my mat. On the mat was where I contemplated being a portal to a great unseen source: All human beings have to pass through the body of a woman before coming to this planet. I'm sure that's why the mother-child bond is as strong as it is.

I now wanted to inspire moms to tap into their pleasures and parent from *that* place! YES I gave birth and YES my life and dreams continued. I've learned from my children and built vast amounts of skills. I'm a mom still on a journey. I gave birth orgasmically to my fourth baby and that's not all, but my body flowed with creation. I had reinvented myself as a mother with a new attitude about motherhood. And so I then gave birth to a business inspiring pleasurable parenting. I gave birth to a new body and mind.

Then the gut punch.

I got a call one evening from my Dad telling me he had to take my mom to the emergency room because she was having difficulty breathing. When I got to the hospital I didn't know what to expect. My mom was seventy-two and my family and I had noticed she was forgetting where she put things, having mood swings, and losing a lot of weight. My parents lived in Buffalo and would drive down often for visits. They were just at my house playing with my children, trying to shoot the basketball in the backyard. A month later I was standing at the door to my mother's hospital room afraid to open the door. She was connected to machines, wore an oxygen mask, and she was sleeping. I stood over her and was flooded with memories of when my mom was healthier. We were really close, like "the only person who got me" kind of close. Her skin felt smooth, soft and warm when I touched her gently, but she was thin and gaunt. Seeing her that way lying in her hospital bed was strange. My mom was known for her curves. When she woke up, I was happy she recognized me immediately. Her recent symptoms and diagnosis of Dementia could have made it impossible. She looked right at me and said, "Hey Kim."

I had absolutely no idea how serious my mother's condition was...could she die from Dementia? At most, my mom had complained about a sore knee with arthritis. She'd never talked about anything else. My family and I stayed with her for ten days, mostly waiting for a diagnosis. We needed to find out what was going on with her. My dad had taken her to the emergency room because she was having trouble breathing. She was too frail for the doctors to perform tests on her. She had surgery to remove fluid that was collecting in her lungs. When they tested the cells in the fluid they found she had lung cancer, colon cancer, and lymphoma. It took all the courage I had to ask the doctors how long my mother was going to live. I thought the doctor would say a few months (they always say three to six months in the movies.) *Oh God, what if they say, six weeks? That I couldn't bear. She was just at my house playing basketball.*

The doctors said, "By the end of the day, or maybe twenty-four hours." The good news was she lived thirty-six hours.

I remember when I left the hospital after my mom passed. I knew I was different; the sun seemed brighter, my eyes hurt, every single part of my body hurt from this sudden loss. I couldn't imagine living in a world without a mother. I wanted to die, too. I got back home and sat on my couch. I didn't do yoga, I cooked when I had to, my children were wonderful and began rapidly maturing because I was a shell of myself. The scary thing about depression is you don't always know you're depressed until you're not. At least that's how I felt.

The pain in my body was an indicator: I needed healing and I was suffering. I went into my new safe sanctuary, the attic, and tried to forget the memories. I wanted to numb the pain of the death of my mom. I wanted to forget who I was and disconnect from everything and everyone. I drank a bottle of wine each day, isolated myself from my friends...*pleasure who, what?* I felt like a failure because I was angry, frustrated, hopeless, and helpless again. I had literally moved into the attic where I had felt trapped. I forgot all my "Zen" training and self-help books and programs. I longed for one more moment with my mom...just one more moment. Then I would cry because I knew I would never have one of those moments again.

I started thinking about my own mortality. What had I accomplished? What have I done? Was being a pleasured mom going to be my biggest accomplishment or was there more I wanted to do, be, and know? I was shaken to my core. My dreams felt fleeting and all I wanted to do was grieve. I decided to do just that...grieve. It was a daring idea, because I was not fine and I decided to be with it and express it.

I cried, hibernated, gained thirty pounds from eating unhealthy foods and drinking everyday—and found myself right for doing it all. *That was exactly where I needed to be to find me.* I would stare in the mirror, going back and forth between memories of my Momma and ask myself over and over and over again, "Who are you?" At first I couldn't answer because I didn't know. But, I knew who and what I was *not*. I was not my jewelry, so I would take that off. I wasn't my make up...my clothes...pretty soon I would be standing in front of the mirror completely naked. Staring at every single curve, scar, mole, blemish, ashy body part, and flaw. I also saw my Momma's hips, her legs, her arms for sure, and her smile. I soon started to see a map of my entire life connecting in my joints. I saw my struggles and successes in my muscles, self care in my toes. I saw desire and longing in my Pussy. Standing there naked looking at myself like I was an explorer charting new land, getting to know the raw naked truth of myself in my sanctuary, in my reflection, is where I fell in love with my nakedness...my sacred nakedness.

After my mother's death, I was changed on a cellular level. Women bleed for about seven days every month but we don't die—we are living breathing miracles. After the b and when I began doing Mama Gena's programs—before my momma transitioned—I began to hear a little voice in my head on my yoga mat. It would whisper, "To be a woman is magickal."

Every single human being on this planet had to pass through a woman's body. We are portals for the unseen divine.

Being a woman is an honor. I believe women are an expression of balance in existence. I felt like my mom was a resource from an unknown spiritual place or perhaps consciousness, teaching me to appreciate myself in a new way. Preparing me for my ascension.

Ascension is defined as "the act of rising to an important position or a higher level". I was experiencing a rebirth after a long sadness and I knew it was going to inspire other women. I got back out into the world with a new passion—being naked and in my power. I started practicing yoga again, alone, in my attic, and naked as the day I was reborn. My naked yoga practice had become a sacred ritual for me—a healing therapy in my private time. I took my clothes off in my attic and didn't want to put them back on. I thought I would be provocative when I decided to post, on Facebook, for April fool's day that I was going to start teaching Naked Yoga on a Beach in New Jersey. I got comments, emails, even texts from over thirty women who actually wanted to do a naked yoga class and they were hoping the post was not a joke.

Those requests made me realize the missing piece of my new healing practice: the magical way that women, when witnessing each other's evolution and radiance, can help each other recover from trauma. I needed sisterhood to witness how I was recreating myself instead of hating or doubting myself. The responses I received revealed other women's desire to be seen and heard in their naked truths, too. Our *bodies* are not the problem. It's the *stories we believe* about our bodies that are the problem. The body is not the abuser, the shamer, or the negative self talk. The Body is a created form that functions based on it's form. However, society, monetary greed, patriarchy, white that supremacy, and privilege all judge our female form by how much money can be made off of exploiting our disgust for our bodies.

For me, it's simple. Can my stomach digest food? Then it is perfect. Can my arm lift things? Then who cares if I have loose skin on my upper arms?

Can my legs move and walk? Yes? Then what is the purpose of a thigh gap? Who is profiting from the destructive stories we play in our psyche over and over again, like a rerun of a show on a canceled network?

My body is my humble servant carrying me on my soul's journey. My body is sacred and divine by design and all women needed to know that life passes through us and we are givers of life—we are reverent. As our heart beats, hips move, and spine lengthens we are radiating energy that inspires human evolution. I feel this as deeply as one can feel truth in the place in my body where there is knowing! If a rose and a lily are in a garden together a rose will never tell a lily to stop being fragrant because it is too much. The same goes for the lily. It's ridiculous to imagine a lily telling a rose to stop being vibrant and multicolored. Rose and Lily would never argue about being *too much*. The rose and lily are in a garden both trying to grow, to potentialize from a small seed. Women, too, are like flowers in the garden of Earth, growing into our best selves.

I didn't think I could come back from such great sadness, but I did. I let my body be my guide—my way back to me and the pleasure and grief of life—feeling the pain and purpose of my body. My humble servant had carried me through every experience on life's journey.

Now, I understand the concept of the body being a temple. More precisely, my body is my place of worship, prayer and connection to source...to God and Goddess. I learned to go within my body to feel safe, loved, and free. My body is the portal between an unseen place of creation and our physical planet. I was reborn. By looking at myself naked in the mirror everyday for months I found peace, healing, and loved the messy sloppy truth. My body was now my sanctuary, my temple and I could finally come out of the attic.

Within three years I experienced an orgasmic birth, the death of my supportive Momma, and the rebirth of something new and outrageous— just because it felt good in my body and for my body. I was alive and living NAKED YOGA, and this practice made me feel more safe, loved, and free than I had ever been. I had something to offer the world...who knew? I dared to get back into life.

We all need healing, and my prayer is that all women remember that we are divine by design. Our bodies are not just for sex and reproduction, but are holy temples of pleasure, desire, and pain. As Mama Gena says, "Women are divinity in the flesh." This is why I say to you, Naked Yoga Goddess, "Bring sacredness to your nakedness."

Kimberly Simms first started doing Yoga in her living room with Rodney Yee DVDs, in 2000, because that was the only way she could afford Yoga. Those videos inspired a new way of life, focus, and thought. She's certified in Bikram and Vinyasa Yoga she likes to joke, she can "hold and flow." Kim believes Yoga keeps her connected, rooted, and open to Divinity. Yoga: the union of mind, body, and breath, brings  alignment and synchronicity into her life. Naked mirror work was an intuitive practice Kim used to help her find her way back to herself after the sudden transition of her mother. Being naked and practicing Yoga joined together became a tool, her map, through the labyrinth of life's journey. A way back to remembering "Self." On her Yoga mat, she learned to slow down and look at life...pose by pose.

Special Gift

My gift to you is a choice of Rose, Lavender, or Lemongrass anointing sprays. I use these sprays during my Naked Yoga Experiences as sacred aromatherapy. The rose energetically opens the Heart Chakra. The Lavender relaxes and soothes energy, and the Lemongrass spray exhilarates the skin and activates the solar plexus—our energy center. Use these sprays as fragrances on your naked body, in your bath, during ceremonies and rituals, or to bless your space. There's positive energy flowing through each bottle. To receive your gift, email me at **nakedyogagoddess@ gmail.com** and let me know what scent you'd like. If you have another intuitive way of using these sacred sprays, I would love to hear your experience! Enjoy!
—THE NAKED YOGA GODDESS

Shifting your Perspective for the Next Generation

BY KATIE SULLIVAN

As women, we have the power to enact change. We see this over and over in the big picture from voting, to marching, to increasing awareness via the #metoo movement. We are hardwired to nurture and protect. We have shown over and over again that we have the power to impact our communities, our government, and the people around us. We strive to set a good example, be a role model, and have a positive influence on those around us.

Within this power and awareness, we also understand the truth in the statement that if you want to change the world, love your family. Just as we actively work on self-love, we strive to teach our daughters to love themselves. My friends who are not mothers do the same in the lives of those young girls and women whom they come in contact with via their community, work, and social circles. We tell them they are beautiful and that they can achieve anything. We believe every positive, encouraging word we share, but are they believing it? The answer to this question lies in what else they are seeing and hearing, and it begs us to get very, very honest with ourselves.

We can't convincingly pass on to others what we don't possess ourselves. To put it in plain terms, never has not just owning but believing our own positive body image been more important, because the messages they are receiving are mixed and the messages are everywhere. A quick visit to Instagram has the power to make even the most confident woman doubt her self-worth, abilities, and appearance. Imagine the pressure for a teen or preteen to "be pretty," "be thin," "be perfect." So how do we combat these messages? How do we help our daughters or younger females within our reach to navigate a society whose beauty standard has, let's face it, gone off the rails? While the answer to that question certainly journeys through healthy social media limits and usage, it starts somewhere else. It starts with us loving ourselves.

Think about this. We eat like we love ourselves and get to yoga or the gym. We strive to be a positive influence. We believe we are setting a good example. We tell our daughters they are beautiful...perfect, even...just the way they are. But our daughter sees us frown when we look at ourselves in the mirror. Maybe she hears us make an offhand or under-our-breath comment that we hate our nose or something about our body. But if this same daughter has been told they look "just like their mother," there will be conflict in what to believe. We are overlooking the power that our words have on their doubt if we assume they will believe us when we tell them they are beautiful with the same features that we don't like about our own selves.

It is important to be aware of where our own body image insecurities are so that we can address them. We address them by accepting our selves and loving ourselves unconditionally. When we achieve that, then we become a warrior for the young women in our lives.

When we love every part of ourselves, we can then speak from a place of power and believability when we tell a younger woman that she can and should do the same. We don't take financial advice from those whose finances are in chaos and we don't take relationship advice from those whose personal lives are a hot mess. So why would we expect anyone to believe us when we tell them they are beautiful, perfect, or a force if we don't have that same belief about ourselves? Quite simply, we cannot.

This is not to say that we do not promote or exemplify humbleness or vulnerability (also good qualities to teach a younger generation) but when it comes to positive body image, there are a lot of people fighting for a young girl's attention and belief system including peers, members of the opposite sex, the entertainment industry, print publications, and every possible social media outlet. That is a lot of noise, so we need to make sure our voice is heard.

How can we do this? First and foremost, we need to watch our words. The ones spoken and unspoken. We need to speak loving thoughts to ourselves so that we do not get caught up in our own insecurities, and we need to be aware of the words we are speaking to ourselves out loud that can be overheard by the younger generation we live with. We need to let those younger than us catch ourselves loving ourselves unconditionally so that they can have the power to do the same, and we need to take the time to encourage those around us, to help them see past their body insecurities.

We can also teach (and improve our own) positive body image by curating a better social media presence. Shortly after joining Instagram, I realized that I wasn't feeling very good about my yoga practice. I had started following the most popular yoga accounts. It was easy to compare where I was in my yoga journey with where other women were in theirs—other women who probably weren't in their late forties with five children. It wasn't in my ability at that time to realize it wasn't a fair comparison I was making. It took the time and effort of doing my own inner work to be able to appreciate my journey independently, without comparing it to others.

We can also teach and improve our own positive body image by understanding that body image—what we look like and how we feel about it—is just one small aspect of our being. We would be remiss if we forgot, even for a second, the beauty of our own intelligence and kindness. We can further tie this to social media by remembering what we want out of social media. We can follow smart accounts that make us think. We can follow encouraging accounts that remind us there are good people in the world. Feed all aspects of your being within your social media: accounts that encourage connection, intelligence, and empathy—not just aesthetic—and encourage the young females in your life to do the same.

Lastly, remember those three words that make most people quake: *Address your trauma.*

It's called inner "work" and not inner "fun" for a reason. It's messy and hard and for some can be very triggering, but to truly love ourselves it is non-negotiable.

To love ourselves, we have to honor every part of ourselves, every experience. The key word is *honor*. We don't have to love those things that we have been through, but we can honor ourselves and our strength in making it through them. We can honor the journey we have had that has made us the woman we presently are.

Why is this shift important? When we love and accept both our inside and our outside, we can then meet others from a place of authenticity when we tell them they are beautiful, powerful females just the way they are. When we are able to impact younger females in this way, we encourage a female narrative that is both as strong as it is loving. Females who love themselves do not perpetuate pettiness among female company. Females who love themselves do not equate attention from boys or men as a measure of their self-worth. Females who love themselves initiate a ripple effect that will impact not just the "next" generation but future generations.

As a mother of three daughters, including a ballerina in a pre-professional program, my ability to teach my daughters to have a healthy body image is an ongoing priority. I understand that my success in this area will affect their current and future health, self- worth, and relationships. I understand this because learning to love myself unconditionally, inside and out, positively affected my own heath, self-worth, and relationships. Accepting and then learning to love (it's a process) my self-perceived flaws made me a happier person. Addressing negatives in my past in a healthy and loving environment where I had both guidance and support, enabled me to not only love myself fully, but to love those around me better. Switching both the how and the how much of my social media usage gave me insight into what I wanted social media interaction to add to my life and what I would not tolerate it adding.

The journey for my daughters to be taught and to have positive body image started with my own. When I shifted my perspective, I had something positive and authentic to say. Something worth listening to.

Katie Sullivan M.S., SLP-CCC, RYT-200 is a speech pathologist, yogi, certified life coach, and blogger who is striving to raise five children including three daughters, with healthy self esteem and body image. You can connect with her at **www.meetvirginiablog. com** where she shares lifestyle, fitness, and humor in surviving life's daily struggles. You can also find her on Instagram **@meetvirginiablog**

The Wisdom of the Fibroid

BY DR. MARA SUSSMAN

This is what radical, unrelenting self love looks like: Practicing it **every... single...day.** Self love no matter what. Self care to save my life.

*One second I'm with a partner who I thought had my back—
then the next, I'm alone.*

I am a healer—a Doctor of Chiropractic since 1999, in private practice since 2005, and certified in pediatrics and pregnancy. In fact, my office was in the only freestanding birth center in the state of Connecticut and the surrounding states!

My journey as a healer has paralleled that of my patients—what they had, I had. All of my experiences were mirrored in them and were for them so that I could help support them at deeper levels.

In *Women's Bodies, Women's Wisdom,* Christiane Northrup (M.D., gynecologist, healer, author, Goddess!) says that fibroid tumors are benign (non-cancerous) tumors of the uterus. They are measured based on what week of pregnancy the uterus is measuring at.

*The fibroids that were inside me were making my uterus appear
to be 16 weeks pregnant.*

It is conservatively estimated that 20-50% of all women in this country have fibroid tumors in their uterus. In *Anatomy of the Spirit,* Caroline Myss (medical intuitive, author, Goddess!) teaches that fibroids are often associated with how we as women express our creativity, or don't! Fibroids are connected to conflicts about creativity, reproduction, and relationships.

I had been a dancer...a free spirit...
it had been shut down little by little until it was non-existent...

In *You Can Heal Your Life*, Louise Hay (Healer, Author, Goddess!) says that fibroids have to do with nursing a hurt from a partner and a blow to the feminine ego.

I had been divorced...then my boys wanted to live with their
Dad...all blows to my female ego...

In *The Secret Language of your Body,* Inna Segal (medical intuitive, healer, author, Goddess!) says fibroids are about holding on to hurts and regrets from the past. Secretly wanting revenge...Feeling disempowered and victimized, forced into things you don't want to do.

I felt out of control...overwhelmed...treated horribly and forced
into not having my boys with me anymore...

It's January, 2017 and I have been having symptoms for 6
months...maybe longer. I have a cute, sweet, annoying buddha
belly—that I pretty much have always had, more or less. In this
case, definitely more. And it's not shrinking no matter what
I eat. None of my "tricks" are working to get it to go down.
Hmmmmm...And then there's this not being able to hold my pee
thing and going more frequently, plus very heavy periods that
are more frequent and last longer...unpredictable...I need to be
checked by a midwife.

I had an ultrasound by a Doctor of Osteopathy because the midwife was not available. This lady had studied and done an internship at the Birth Center where I practiced so that felt like a sign that I was in the right place. And she also knew the midwife who took care of me and helped me birth both my boys. So I relaxed...a little.

She told me she couldn't visualize my left ovary as it was so covered in tumors and that my whole uterine cavity was filled. She said the solution was a hysterectomy. I went blank...shock...

I left her office.

I cried...freaked out...couldn't speak...screamed...felt betrayed...HOW COULD THIS HAPPEN TO ME?

And then I called all of my healers.

My deep belief has always been this: *If my body can make something, it can also unmake it.*

I knew this challenge. This seeming "problem" was actually a messenger from my soul—a redirection of my path. A tremendous opportunity to heal and understand me, myself, and I on deeper levels. And I was ready.

THE FIBROID IS A MICROCOSM OF THE MACROCOSM

It has felt like a flower shedding its petals; sometimes gently, sometimes like a pounding rainstorm has obliterated it. I have had meditation dreams of it where the petals come off and form a beautiful mandala, signifying wholeness and taking up space—in a BIG way. Not stuffing feelings into my uterus anymore. And creating...a huge ball of toxic feelings and a bloody mess!

I used to stay in the positive, in a fantasy, in the easy. I was the Queen of spinning situations into being "okay"—workable. And I then put the real hard, dark feelings into my uterus. No one could see them there, including me. This way I was acceptable...easy going...and I could "handle" all that came at me—for a time.

I feel my uterus now. When I am floating in the sensory deprivation chamber at my local float center, I put my hands right on her and hold her. It always feels different to me. Sometimes she's a cute little ball and I say, "Hi." I'll practice saying, "I love you," too. Sometimes truly meaning it, sometimes not.

Sometimes I feel my uterus and it is barely there, and I wonder if the fibroids are all completely gone. And then I let go of that because it doesn't really matter. I *know* I am healthy in my energetics and that is where I am on my path. The physical is the last phase of body dysfunction and so what shows up there is older information. As I now change my vibration and love myself in a deeper way, the physical will catch up to the soul and the energetics. Now eighteen months later, the symptoms are gone and my health is super vibrant. I feel my signals clearly, although it is a daily practice.

What does *fibroid* represent to me? It represents the essence of femininity, of women's collective experience so far here on this planet. The container of the divine feminine. What happens to me, happens to you and what happens to you, happens to me. (There really is only one of us here—we are that connected.) Fibroids are built slowly over time. They have memories and hold a very strong energy. They stop the flow in the uterus and make it hard or impossible for a baby to implant into the wall of the uterus. They also make it hard for us to be creative, or to create in any way.

The fibroids actually saved me and saved my unborn child from being in a destructive and manipulative relationship for longer than was necessary to learn the lessons and move on. You see, in my second marriage we had really wanted to get pregnant. We got pregnant twice during our relationship, but I couldn't hold either pregnancy—and now I know why. I am eternally grateful for the sacred wisdom of my body, knowing before me and keeping me safe and planning my glorious future all by herself, without my personality and ego getting involved.

That is my soul and the divine feminine in *fucking* action.

It all started out feeling like confusion. In my first marriage, my husband's reactions to my behavior would change unexpectedly without warning or understanding on my part. And then there was yelling, and never answers to my questions or even a discussion about it was allowed.

> *I became a beautiful pretzel*
> *I tied myself into knots*
> *all the way down to my uterus*
> *Trying to anticipate all of the needs of everyone*
> *trying to please him*
> *And the kids*
> *And never knowing how or why or what*
> *I just started to feel so confused*
> *And was totally disconnected from knowing me*

Then I had a "routine" PAP smear—I had abnormal cells in my cervix. And then I knew: Me, as I am right now, will not survive this relationship. I had a super strong intuitive feeling that it was my relationship in my cervix and uterus and that the abnormal cells were the microcosm of my dysfunctional macrocosm of my life at that time...Keeping all of my anger, hurt, resentment, TRUTH...Down deep inside me...hiding...

This realization started me on this part of my sacred journey, and in that moment of realization, I chose MYSELF—not my relationship, not my partner, not my kids. I chose me. And I somehow knew that all would be served if I was healthy—on ALL levels: Physical, Chemical, Mental, Emotional, Spiritual, and on a Soul's level.

But how was I to do this? I started doing what I wanted, whatever I was interested in, whatever seemed fun, exciting, pleasurable...whatever felt like nourishment to my soul. I read lots of books and sought out healers in all forms. I started creating boundaries, listening to my body/feelings/emotions more actively and with more reverence. Getting quiet, meditating in order to listen...sitting in the uncomfortable places of my perceived failures...what my parents expected...my husband...my kids...my friends.

I began noticing when I was working on my patients that I would have some physical manifestations come up in me. I had never noticed this in the past, but now, I was experiencing things like clearing my throat, coughing, yawning, and getting the chills. I started paying attention to them and realized they were all communication from my soul, from my patient's soul, from our guides and angels...from the Divine. This changed EVERYTHING! It all became so much more exciting, intriguing, and effective. The awareness and tuning in helped me to become better at my healing craft.

I practiced this everyday, allowing myself to feel and follow my body more and my brain less. It was very challenging for me, since I'd been taught the polar opposite.

I would discuss and suggest these same ideas to my patients and we all learned together, turning health challenges into journeys of discovery, opportunities for understanding, and possibilities for deeper self knowledge, love and wisdom.

Also, there was huge disappointment, frustration, upset, self-questioning and self-loathing at times, when the "answers" weren't obvious or coming in a form I understood...when health got worse...when the unexpected happened...when babies died...moms died...when suffering was all around us.

*How could I have created a fibroid that was the size of a 16
week pregnancy? How could I have had all of these symptoms
for eighteen months and longer...and ignored them? Discounted
them, hid them, and pretended not to notice them for soooo
fucking long? How could I be so seemingly happy, and yet be
growing this uncontrollable mass in my womb? Ughhh—haven't
I learned enough? Gone through enough?*

So, yeah. I had my moments of huge self doubt, worry, all the unknowns.
And I had huge gratitude for it all, too; for seeing the obstacle and realizing that the fibroid was the way for me—it held the answers. My body and
soul together held the answers, even when I was bypassing and going in the
wrong direction in some areas of my life. She re-directed me, clearly and
powerfully. Protecting me. Keeping me safe. Keeping me here.

I held my hands over her and cried...and cried...and held her. I wanted
her to be a baby, not a fibroid. I wanted my belly to be flat. I wanted to be
able have a larger bladder. I wanted to feel sexy. I wanted to have smooth,
flowing, predictable monthly cycles.

What I did was *let the fuck go*...and surrendered.

I went to my dear friend and Shaman/Healer for help, as well as many
other intuitive, magical beings, healers, coaches, mentors, and friends...and
started the process of peeling the layers of this mass by taking the petals off
one by one, and opening to learn a new way...again.

I usually don't remember my dreams, but one particular day I did. I
dreamed that my older son had died. I didn't tell anyone. My insides froze
up. I couldn't go there, or even allow myself to think or journal about it. So
I left it.

Two weeks later during a meditation I received a vision of many more
layers of the fibroid shedding and leaving, all with my older son's DNA—all
of his contribution. I can feel that my relationships with all the men in my
life have all contributed in some way to this piece of art in my uterus.Overtly,
covertly, consciously, unconsciously...

From this life, past lives, parallel lives...Sometimes I can feel what is
leaving and sometimes I can't, depending on what is going on in my life at
the time. So all the pieces of the fibroid were all the men in my life and how
I chose to manage each of their relationships. From when I was newly incar-

nated and still in my mother's womb. How I stuffed my feelings and wanted everyone to be happy in my divorced family. Being the first child and taking that role of keeping everyone protected and okay. Continuing with that and bringing it into my first marriage—everyone happy, everyone handled, everything anticipated, *everything planned out* was my mantra. Then with my second marriage realizing there were even deeper issues of self-betrayal and self-sabotage going on, because they had to be going on in the microcosm for them to be happening in the macrocosm.

This gave me so much insight and strength for when my second marriage started to falter. I woke up, and stood up, and confronted, and refused to sacrifice myself again, in record time.

And so I was able to change course again and come back into this version of alignment.

By trusting my own deep wisdom and the subsequent strength and courage from the process, I have grown from being nothing, to being my everything.

Thank you for being a part of my sacred journey by reading my work...
I am super grateful and hope it serves you and your community in a big way.
—Mara

Dr. Mara Sussman is a seeker, healer, Chiropractor since 1999, momma of two extraordinary teenage boys, a dog and a cat, and a step-momma to an amazing and wise woman. She is an author, coach, speaker, mentor, Reiki practitioner, yogi, dancer, channeler, and intuitive. Mara is an educator and enthusiast of essential Oils, and a passionate seeker of freedom for ALL  through exceptional health and vitality on every level: Physical, Chemical, Mental, Emotional, Spiritual, and Energetic.

Mara's awakening occurred through her pregnancies with her boys as well as through countless healings, her patients, relationships, family, friends, and kindred sister goddess souls. She has persistently pursued her souls work—to reminding beings of self love, divine freedom, and their own inner divine truth.

Mara has found that symptoms of all kinds are informational and communication from SOUL which help lead us on our sacred journeys. She supports other in translating these signs and symptoms for the benefit of ALL of us. Mara believes that we are here with our genius contributions, talents, and soul's work. As we get closer to and clearer about fulfilling our sacred work, we heal ourselves, our communities our countries, our planet, our galaxy, our Universe...and beyond. This brings us all to a beautiful state of bliss. Learn more at **www.drmara.net.**

The EmBODY Codes: Transmissions of a Mystic on the Wisdom of the Sacred Body and Being Human

BY PATRICIA WALD-HOPKINS

There is never enough time to live, Beloved, in this time of
Human-ness.
Dance Sister.
Dance Brother.
Alone and in union.
Celebrate this Human Body like it is the Temple of the Sun and
the Moon and the Stars.
Honor it because It came from Heaven.
The Holy Body of the Flesh Is the Sacred Temple of the Soul.
Embody it in totality, yet let it not be a prison
So tether me, please, ever so lightly to this Earth
That I may be in Service in all the Divine and Human ways I
am designed to be.
Let me rest gently the soles of my feet upon the richness of this
Earth plane
And use my Body to weave a most spectacular Light show into
what we call Life.
This is my story of how a Mystic found Her Way home into her
Body
How She has come to truly inhabit Her Physicality on Earth.
To devour the Essence of Life through her senses
And activate her cellular connectivity to Humanity.
Let the rain soften my heart.
Let the damp air breathe life into my body.
Let the thunder awaken my soul's true Desire.
I am tentative and I am whole.
I am gentle and I am ferociously compassionate about my life.
Let the darkness turn to light by showing up for mySELF in the
Mystery and the Mundane each and every day.
Amen.

WHAT IS THE SACRED BODY?

The Sacred Body is the crystalline architecture of the flesh and bone we call our human Body. It is the divine architecture: the subatomic, atomic parts and the cellular matrix from which we take physical form. It is what we are designed from, and it is not of this world. It is stardust incarnate in a certain form unique to each one of us in a physical form.

WHAT IS THE WISDOM OF THE SACRED BODY?

Sacred Body Wisdom is the innate intelligence of our cells, tissues, and chemistry independent of our thinking. It is your Body Deva. It knows, without logic, what it needs to thrive on this planet. The mind as we know it is a tool to acquire the things we need to be nourished and to thrive.

PHASES OF EMBODIMENT

The Pain Body > The Emotional Body > The Spiritual Body

PHASE 1 (THE PAIN BODY): TENDER ROOTS—THE LONGING FOR BELONGING—THE YEARS LOST IN SEEKING

By the time I reached my mid-thirties, the tender wounds of youth had led my whole Being into the raging and purifying fires of Kali Ma. I'd spent nearly two decades behind the veil of an intellectual seeking to fill my hunger for the long lost God of my childhood. I sought knowledge, I sought the stories of other worlds and lives, and I sought the ends of the Earth to see as much of it as I could in a desperate attempt to fill the void of spirituality in my life. As a young person, I was always happiest lost in the pages of a book or the spaciousness of nature. A wildness in my Being sought refuge in these places from the hard edges of cultural rules. The undefinable nature of a free spirit lay dormant within me like a sleeping dragon waiting patiently for the time in my life she could be truly free.

I was born and raised as a Catholic, from a middle-class family in the rural sacredness of Santa Fe, New Mexico. I am flesh and blood of northern New Mexico. I was born Patricia Librada Gallegos, and I am the youngest of four children in a traditional northern New Mexican Hispanic family. I grew up in a place where the land is wide open and filled with enchantment in the midst of socioeconomic disparity. I'm pretty certain that is why I chose to incarnate in this place—for its closeness to the raw earth and humanity. When I was young, I didn't know why I was here, I just was...and I was fairly certain I was never going to survive the pressure of society to look and be a certain way. I eventually poised myself from the awkwardness of my childhood into a smart, athletic girl with a very curious quietness. I preferred to be alone in my own thoughts. I preferred running for endless miles over connecting and hanging out in groups. I wanted to be with the abstract and the wildness. That magical whispering wind. The dew on the blades of grass. The mist in the mountains. These were the things that made me feel most alive in my body. The movement. The senses activated. A melancholic compassion always filled my heart, but was tucked away like a sacred secret for another time. I look back now and I see I was a very twisted piece of work. A split personality. The outside constructed by pure force and willpower and the insides of my aching heart subdued by the mental and physical distraction to be a certain way.

I starved my body and worked her relentlessly into a form I felt fit in with the norm and would secure me a safe place in society. I had a voracious mind and I fed her as much as I could. I pursued degrees in biology and environmental health and toxicology because I loved the study, but it also gave me a safe place to be. I also had a huge appetite for adrenaline and pushing myself to the edge of life. Mountain climbing, rock climbing, bicycle racing, marathons...This is how I justified being human because when I sat with my heart, she really didn't want any of this life. I was in psychotherapy from age sixteen to twenty-three and then again at thirty-five. When transitions came, life was just too much for me. I often felt I was too much for life with all my feelings. I continued doing everything I could do to keep from actually feeling who I was and knowing my SELF. Anorexia/bulimia, exercise-aholism, and work-aholsim all kept me from dropping into myself and truly knowing myself—and yet it all kept me from leaving this earth plane too soon. I was suicidal in my teens and early twenties, ungrounded and unconnected to anything until I found Gaia in the high mountains and the Pacific Ocean. I spent free time in Colorado, Utah, Wyoming, Montana, Washington, and Oregon. I traveled to sacred places in Mexico, Peru, Ecuador, France, Spain, and the Himalayas. If it had not been for the places of magical sanctuary on this Earth, I would have given up long ago on this human thing. Left without a trace.

I raced. I raced as a runner, falling in love with long distances and scenic marathons and half marathons. I raced as a bicyclist excelling in hill climbs, time trials, and duathlons (bike/run). I raced in cross-country skiing, climbing mountains and trekking in so many beautiful places. My body loved the physical exertion.

I spent about fifteen years in this phase, and I still longed for more. Life had to be more than escapades.

PHASE 2 (THE EMOTIONAL BODY): MOTHERHOOD—THE TIME OF CHAOS - THE TIME OF METAMORPHOSIS

About this time I left my first long-term relationship of fifteen years, quit my corporate job, and went to massage school. My life changed dramatically from left-brained to right-brained. No easy transition! I found myself in many dark nights of the soul as I sorted through what was self and not self. This time of chaos was also a great time of creation. All the energy I had been cranking out in physical and mental power turned to a new relationship and creating three babies in a span of four years. The most exhausting and gratifying years of my life opened to me through the initiation of motherhood, moving me through a passage from selfishness to selflessness and then to a point of wholeness once again.

This journey into motherhood began when I was thirty-seven. My whole life rearranged. All my pure force embodiment practices ceased to work. I was forced into an alchemical cocoon of transformation, and that is where I have been for the last ten years—in a cosmic soup of my own evolution. This opened a direct portal for me to Spirit. I devoured anything to do with Spirit, and my healing business grew with bodywork, energy healing, coaching, spiritual groups, and healing art.

It was the creative process I accessed through my healing journey that brought the EmBODY codes into my cellular matrix. I am an alchemical weaver of energies, using sound, movement, and nature sanctuary to call into creation digital imagery art, essential oil perfumes, and crystals alchemy that access frequencies of higher consciousness and activate the cellular and genetic matrix to that plane of existence that I didn't know existed before, except in a state of complete adrenaline rush and post-endorphine flood from extreme exercise or exertion.

I found the power of my voice in my belly and in my hands and my whole body. I create art and sacred space for life from these languages of light—frequencies brought through from Spirit. I know some will balk at this process of being a channel for Spirit and a conduit for frequencies of Higher Consciousness. Some may stand in disbelief that any of my creations could serve as a portal to receive the transmissions I receive from Spirit. The transmissions I receive are the emBODY codes. I am here to master being human and to share all I can with the world as I reach my own higher levels of self-mastery. The way I share the codes is through my art and through one-on-one work with people using my voice and hands to transfer the codes. I have learned how to use sacred dance, kundalini yoga, and contemplation to access the codes and manifest them into three-dimensional art and processes. I am a shamanic practitioner and curator of all things esoteric. I use the Akashic Records, Gene Keys, and Human Design to navigate the matrix and find alignment with my Divine Design and support others to do the same. And this leaves me at the doorway of the next phase of my life. The one where I really "get" at a cellular level why I am here and how I may share my sacred work with the world.

PHASE 3 (THE SPIRITUAL BODY): ENTER MENOPAUSE—THE MASTER OF THE MATRIX - THE CREATRIX

I don't have the answers to Life nor do I need them anymore
I have a feeling
A sense of direction that comes from a wordless place
Whispers in the wind
Rain falling
Damp air
Essence of sage in the morning air
The highlights of gold in my son's hair
The sea of green in my daughter's eyes
The sound of my husband's voice
Endless codes of embodiment come through my senses
Creating presence and a field of grace from which to set foot in each day
I am not here to be somebody great or special
I am here to love wholeheartedly this gift of life
To feel the deepest emotions of sadness, rage, and joy and remain a
sound vessel for creation of beauty in this world through my hands, my voice,

my entire body, because the human body is a force of light at play in this divine leela (play)
Embodiment is to be of this world and not of this world all at the same time.
To use your mind to serve the heart that is being led by Spirit.

I enter into this next phase of life seeking to be a leader of spiritual liberation so that our hearts may be open and our bodies free from the oppression of the mind and filled with joy. Free from the old programming and the obsolete biochemical cascades, free to fully occupy my Voice as a writer and inspirational muse of the leaders of our future, the children and the child within each one of us. I humbly stand at this next portal of initiations as my body continues to be purified by my own internal biochemical fire of perimenopause to menopause.

I fully intend to express my soul through my art and all creations. To create sanctuary for sacredness in everyday life. I intend to mend the split between heart and mind in myself, so that all my decisions and actions come from a place of compassion. To find a way to hold my own stewardship of the resources of earth in a way that is sustainable. To find a way to fill my cup to overflow to others.

I am coming to a deep understanding of the process of change. I am not in charge. I am being placed exactly where I need to be for today. My work is to honor and cherish my body and all life as it shows up today. There is delight in all things. And it is in the field of delight that transformation can take place. It is with a joyful heart that we are meant to be human.

I am in deep gratitude to my husband, children, family, and friends, including my sacred sisters and brothers who have walked with me and stood by me through the time of Seeking, Metamorphosis, and now this transition into sacred service as a Master of the Matrix. I am in gratitude to The Gene Keys and the Metamorphix Council members that have held a sacred container for the Great Change to come through us all in an alchemical fire of purification, so that what remains is a pure Light to share in service.

I offer the following rituals and practices that have supported me and my clients from living by force into living from a place of deep inner strength so that life is filled with satisfaction and delight, so that you may live your legendary life through Love:

EMBODY CODE RITUALS AND PRACTICES

- Body Movement/ Dance/Kundalini Yoga
- Voice Work
- Hand Weaving
- Drumming
- Bodywork (massage, craniosacral therapy)
- Energy Healing (Reiki)
- Plant Allies (essential oils, plant medicine)
- Crystal Allies
- Earth Sanctuary (gardens, trekking, temples)
- Healing Art (imagistic contemplations, alchemical perfumes)
- Gene Keys Ambassador
- Human Design Study
- Oracle Card Readings/Akashic Records
- Running, Cycling, Kayaking, Hiking
- Community
- Service

*"Sing to the cells of the sacred body of your human form and
to that of the larger sacred body of earth to create portals of potentiality
for healing and transformation for Humanity and Gaia."*

Patricia (Trish) Wald-Hopkins is a licensed Massage Therapist, Reiki Master, Energy Coach, and Scientist. She has been practicing healing arts since 2008. She also holds a bachelor's degree in Biology and a master's degree in Environmental Health and Toxicology and for more than 20 years has assessed the mechanisms of how environmental stressors, particularly toxins in the environment, affect the  body and the larger ecology. She was a board-certified toxicologist for 10 years and worked in scientific research laboratories and in the corporate world, focusing on the risk assessment of the biochemical and physiological aspects of stress, primarily on ecological systems. Her focus for the last decade has expanded to include exploring the biochemical effects of essential oils and other healing modalities on holistic well-being.

Trish's work combines scientific and intuitive modalities that support you to live a life filled with joy, love, and creativity. She specializes in energy medicine to support your well-being and the manifestation of an enriching lifestyle based on your needs and desires. Trish uses a fusion of hands-on and distance energy medicine techniques and lifestyle coaching. She uses sacred sounds, essential oils, and bodywork to support clearing, healing, and nurturing of the physical body and light body, so that you can be at your highest level of luminosity in all your manifestations and creations on earth.

Trish also creates healing art, sacred spaces, and sanctuary for healing and living by clearing toxic energy from your body and spaces and filling it back up with the good stuff. She spent many years in the laboratory studying the biochemistry of life under environmental stressors, which has supported her alchemy and optimization of lifestyle to nourish the body and find harmony in your environment. Trish also creates alchemical elixirs with essential oils and crystals using high-vibration ingredients to create embodiment support through plant allies. Learn more at **www.mariposabodyandwellness.com.**

Special Gift

Soja Ne Water Goddess of Joy, Love and Vitality Video
Activation Meditation and follow-up lifestyle optimization
assessment call.

Contact Trish at 505-238-6814 or email
trish@mariposabodyandwellness.com to receive your gift!

Additional Books by Flower of Life Press

The Caregiving Journey: Information. Guidance. Inspiration.

The New Feminine Evolutionary: Embody Presence—Become the Change

Pioneering the Path to Prosperity: Discover the Power of True Wealth and Abundance

Emerge: 7 Steps to Transformation (No matter what life throws at you!)

Practice: Wisdom from the Downward Dog

Soul On Fire: Divine Reminders Along the Path of Awakening

Sisterhood of the Mindful Goddess: How to Remove Obstacles, Activate Your Gifts, and Become Your Own Superhero

Path of the Priestess: Discover Your Divine Purpose

Sacred Call of the Ancient Priestess: Birthing a New Feminine Archetype

Rise Above: Free Your Mind—One Brushstroke at a Time

Menopause Mavens: Master the Mystery of Menopause

The Power of Essential Oils: Create Positive Transformation in Your Well-Being, Business, and Life

Self-Made Wellionaire: Get Off Your Ass(et), Reclaim Your Health, and Feel Like a Million Bucks

Oms From the Mat: Breathe, Move, and Awaken to the Power of Yoga

Oms From the Heart: Open Your Heart to the Power of Yoga

The Four Tenets of Love: Open, Activate, and Inspire Your Life's Path

The Fire-Driven Life: Ignite the Fire of Self-Worth, Health, and Happiness with a Plant-Based Diet

Visit us at **www.FlowerofLifepress.com**